FRANK UNDERHILL
AND THE POLITICS OF IDEAS

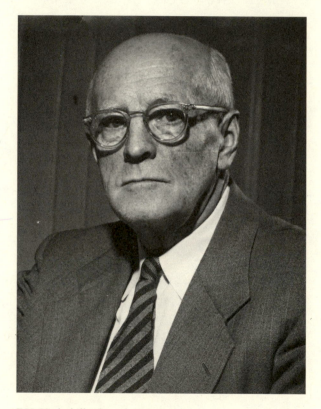

F.H. Underhill (photo by Newton)

Frank Underhill
and the Politics of Ideas

KENNETH C. DEWAR

McGill-Queen's University Press
Montreal & Kingston • London • Ithaca

ISBN 978-0-7735-4487-1 (cloth)
ISBN 978-0-7735-4520-5 (paper)
ISBN 978-0-7735-8260-6 (ePDF)
ISBN 978-0-7735-8261-3 (ePUB)

Legal deposit first quarter 2015
Bibliothèque nationale du Québec

Printed in Canada on acid-free paper that is 100% ancient forest free
(100% post-consumer recycled), processed chlorine free

McGill-Queen's University Press acknowledges the support of the
Canada Council for the Arts for our publishing program. We also
acknowledge the financial support of the Government of Canada
through the Canada Book Fund for our publishing activities.

Library and Archives Canada Cataloguing in Publication

Dewar, Kenneth C. (Kenneth Cameron), 1944–, author
    Frank Underhill and the politics of ideas/Kenneth C. Dewar.

    Includes bibliographical references and index.
    Issued in print and electronic formats.
    ISBN 978-0-7735-4487-1 (bound). – ISBN 978-0-7735-4520-5 (pbk.). –
    ISBN 978-0-7735-8260-6 (ePDF). – ISBN 978-0-7735-8261-3 (ePUB)

    1. Underhill, Frank H., 1889–1971. 2. Underhill, Frank H.,
    1889–1971 – Political and social views. 3. Underhill, Frank H.,
    1889–1971 – Political activity. 4. Historians – Canada – Biography.
    5. Intellectuals – Canada – Biography. 6. College teachers – Canada –
    Biography. 7. Socialists – Canada – Biography. 8. Canada – Politics
    and government – 20th century. I. Title.

FC151.U53D49 2015   971.0072'02 `   C2014-907640-1
                                               C2014-907641-X

This book was typeset by Interscript in 10.5 / 13.5 Sabon.

To Marged

Contents

Acknowledgments

I have incurred many debts in writing this book. I would like to thank the staff at Library and Archives Canada, the University of Toronto Archives, and Mount Saint Vincent University Library for their assistance with my research. Two grants from the Senate Committee on Research and Publications at the Mount were especially helpful in the early stages of the project. I would also like to thank Brook Taylor, dean of Arts and Science at the Mount, for providing me with work space after my retirement in 2011.

The seed of this book was planted in conversations with Blair Neatby at Carleton University in 1981–82, and when it came to fruition (after a long period of dormancy) he read the draft manuscript and made helpful comments. I am very grateful for his help and encouragement. I would also like to thank Terry Copp, Mark Phillips, and Barnett Richling, friends with whom I have discussed different parts of the manuscript over the years, and Brian McKillop, who published my initial forays into Underhill territory in the (sadly short-lived) *Underhill Review*. Other essays were published by *History of Intellectual Culture* and Oxford University Press. I thank all three for their permission to use parts of those essays here. Presentations to groups at the Mount and the Department of History at Carleton University offered opportunities to work out some of my ideas about Frank

Underhill's thought and practice, as did the W.C. Desmond Pacey Memorial Lecture at the University of New Brunswick, which I was invited to give in 2009.

At McGill-Queen's University Press I have appreciated the guidance and assistance of executive director Philip Cercone, managing editor Ryan Van Huijstee, and especially acquisitions editor James MacNevin. Two anonymous readers of the manuscript offered a stimulating combination of encouragement and suggestions for improvement. I hope they will feel I have done justice to their suggestions.

I owe my greatest debt of gratitude to my wife Marged, for both her support and her sound editorial judgment. This book is dedicated to her.

Foreword

BOB RAE

Frank Underhill stands in the forefront of Canada's political activists, essayists, and historians. Ken Dewar has done us all a great favour by placing Underhill's great gifts in the context of the rich political and intellectual history of the twentieth century.

One of Frank Underhill's mentors, Malcolm Wallace, used a phrase that Underhill often borrowed – "Canada's history is as dull as ditchwater and our politics is full of it." The irony is that Underhill's own life and work is proof positive as to how completely untrue that stereotype is. A gifted student at the University of Toronto before the First World War, and then at Balliol College, Oxford, Underhill fought in the war and returned to Canada to teach history, first at the University of Saskatchewan, and then for thirty years at the University of Toronto.

A brilliant teacher and lecturer, Underhill was quickly swept up in the politics and issues of his time. He was an Ontario Grit, a reformer, a radical, a socialist, and yet, as this valuable book makes clear, a liberal and an iconoclast never comfortable embracing what George Orwell memorably called "the smelly little orthodoxies" of his time.

He was one of the drafters of the Regina Manifesto and a founder of the League for Social Reconstruction. A great friend and supporter of J.S. Woodsworth, Underhill never lost his underlying liberalism or his discomfort in any comfortable pew.

He railed against the complacency of a two-party system that was more about "ins" and "outs" than matters of deep principle. Yet after a twenty-five-year association with the Co-operative Commonwealth Federation he began to question the party's discomfort in entering the world of affluence and power politics.

He began voting Liberal again in the early 1960s, and dedicated a book of his essays, *In Search of Canadian Liberalism*, to Lester B. "Mike" Pearson. The Ontario Grit had come home, wiser for the journey, and still full of a love for controversy and spirited debate.

Frank Underhill spent much of his life lamenting his own shortcomings and failures – he never produced his great book on Liberalism, his biography of Edward Blake. As the academy became more compartmentalized, his unwillingness to specialize and write vast tomes put him at odds with his colleagues.

As Ken Dewar's book points out, it seems churlish to complain that Underhill never became something he wasn't. He was a master of the short, sharp essay, and his political journalism was the best there was in the 1930s and '40s. His influence on generations of students was legendary. In short, we should understand him for what he was, and as an act of historical generosity, quietly remove the Puritan monkey on Underhill's back. He might have judged himself harshly. Based on what we see in this book, there is no reason for us to do so.

Indeed it can be said that Underhill was present at the creation of both the CCF and the renewed Liberal Party in opposition in the 1960s. He annoyed party loyalists because he was never afraid to tell what he saw as the truth to power, and if his questioning even led him to disagree with what he had said or written before, so be it. As one of his heroes, George Bernard Shaw, pointed out, "if you can't change your mind, you can't change anything."

Dewar's book also points out the extent of Underhill's courage in the face of repeated efforts by the university administration to discipline him for his political beliefs and, in one infamous episode in the early 1940s, to fire him. No less a figure than Arthur Meighen recommended that he be interned. Never a man of means, he was forced to agree to "behave," but these periods of public silence were happily brief. This reminds us how fragile academic freedom has been at important moments in our history.

On a personal note, in my fourth year in modern history at the University of Toronto in the late 1960s I had the wonderful experience of being in a small seminar, "Canadian Intellectual History," taught by Carl Berger. I wrote my final paper on the League for Social Reconstruction, and began reading Underhill in some depth. I later thought of writing a thesis on Underhill, but life took a different course and eventually I ended up in law school. I met Underhill once, when he came back to U of T to reminisce at the History Department. His humour was impish, his spirit was wry, and his words were wistful. But there was sparkle and a passion always marked by self-deprecation. Ken Dewar has done us all a service by bringing Frank Underhill to life in this book.

FRANK UNDERHILL
AND THE POLITICS OF IDEAS

Prologue

There is no country in the world where intellectuals suffer from such low repute as in Canada.

F.H. Underhill, "Notes on the Massey Report," 1951

Frank Underhill practically invented the role of the intellectual in English-speaking Canada. Born in 1889, he spent his working life as a professor of history, first at the University of Saskatchewan, beginning in 1914, then at Toronto for almost thirty years, from 1927 to 1955. In semi-retirement, he moved to Ottawa, where he served for a time as curator of Laurier House, a kind of archive-*cum*-shrine of the Liberal party, and taught occasionally at Carleton University, until his death in 1971 at the age of 81. Through all these years, Underhill maintained an ambivalent relationship with his chosen profession, sometimes resisting its demands, at other times embracing them. He adopted instead the role of the intellectual, which emerged as a cultural force early in the twentieth century, and whose history paralleled the professionalization of history and other academic disciplines that began just as he was embarking on his career. In choosing public engagement as a writer, speaker, and critic, he created tensions for himself that would shape his life and thought, threaten his career, and help to redefine the nature of academic freedom in Canada. At the same time, he also won wide respect and a good measure of influence – difficult as that might be to calculate – both within his profession and beyond, and did so on his own terms.

The intellectual flourished as a cultural type for many decades, often in the face of adversity; in fact, one could say it flourishes still, though on very different terms than those on which it established itself in the years following World War I. The archetype originated in France in the 1890s, where "intellectual" was first used as a noun – or at least where that usage first took on currency – to describe the critics of the French state in the Dreyfus Affair, the infamous trial and conviction, then exoneration, of a Jewish army officer, Captain Alfred Dreyfus, of espionage on behalf of Germany. Subsequently, the usage spread, especially in the aftermath of the Bolshevik Revolution of 1917, conditioned by broadly left-wing disenchantment with the modern state and by the fears this disenchantment aroused.[1] In the beginning, its novelty was not difficult to spot. In Canada, in 1929, J.S. Woodsworth (1874–1942), the Labour member of Parliament for Winnipeg North Centre (and soon to be the founding leader of the Co-operative Commonwealth Federation, forerunner of the New Democratic Party), placed the term in quotation marks when he proposed to Underhill that the power of "intellectuals" might be harnessed in an organization similar to the socialist Fabian Society in Great Britain. The result was the League for Social Reconstruction (LSR), which Underhill founded, together with the Montreal lawyer and poet F.R. Scott (1899–1985).[2] No one today puts "intellectuals" in quotation marks in everyday usage.

There was nothing new, of course, about reflection on the relation between matters of the mind (or spirit) and matters of the state, a mode of thought that had a long history in the Western tradition. It stretched back through the writings of Voltaire, the French Enlightenment *philosophe*, in the eighteenth century, to the Italian philosopher Marsilius of Padua on the relations of church and state in the early fourteenth century, to Plato in ancient Athens. Canadian thinkers of the generation or two before Underhill included men like the journalist and historian W.D. LeSueur, the philosopher John

Watson, and the physician and essayist Andrew Macphail; their views on politics and social issues were informed by a concern for religion, ethics, and individual morality. They wrote in the manner of the Victorian sage or man of letters.[3] "Intellectuals" were a manifestation of this mode of thought particular to the twentieth century, even to the *short* twentieth century, the years from World War I to the fall of the Berlin Wall and the collapse of the Union of Soviet Socialist Republics in 1989–91, though the question of the end point, or whether there was an end point at all, is much disputed. While intellectuals shared a kinship with earlier figures, they constituted a distinctively modern – and modernist – cultural type, which emerged almost simultaneously everywhere in the Western world and beyond.

They were typically men, at a time when men dominated both the university, which tended to be the base from which intellectuals operated, at least in Canada, and the daily and periodical press, which were their chief means of reaching a wide audience (and, it must be said, of supplementing their moderate incomes). While commonly practising some academic specialty in their professional lives, they tended to have a generalist bent and to value cultural expression in all of its forms. Above all, they believed it was their civic duty to turn whatever expertise they might have to public purposes, and to do so regardless of whether their opinions might elicit assent or opposition. They usually anticipated the latter, rather than the former, and most were self-conscious heretics of one kind or another.[4] Certainly this was true of Underhill, and when he was forced to keep his opinions to himself, if not exactly to recant, at the University of Toronto in the late 1930s and early 1940s, he suffered a humiliation damaging to his health as well as to his self-esteem. Intellectuals, in short, had a sense of alienation from the mainstream of society. This distinguished them from public critics of the immediately preceding generations in the Anglo-American world with whom they otherwise had much in common, but who had tended to regard themselves as leaders of opinion, enjoining their readers to act on ideals that they all shared. The intellectuals of Underhill's time were, by contrast, disaffected outsiders. Of all their nineteenth-century forebears, perhaps the closest in attitude and outlook were the radical critics of the Russian intelligentsia.

The primary focus of Underhill's public commentary was national politics. Here, too, he both led and exemplified change. After the CCF was founded in 1932, Woodsworth sought to place the party on a sound and sophisticated ideological foundation, and he turned to members of the LSR for assistance. Underhill wrote the first draft of what became the Regina Manifesto, the party platform adopted at the first national convention of the CCF, held in July 1933 in the prairie city for which it was named. Subsequently, he threw himself into party organization and promotion, giving talks and leading educational study groups aimed at demonstrating the need for the establishment of a "co-operative commonwealth" in Canada and showing just what form it might take. He also wrote prolifically, especially in the *Canadian Forum*, the left-wing journal of opinion where he mainly established his reputation as an intellectual. Yet, having laid a claim to a place among the founders of modern parliamentary socialism in Canada, Underhill became disenchanted with the CCF, especially with those of its leaders who put vote-getting before the propagation of reform ideas, however they might be put into practice, and with those who failed to recognize the dangers of a too-powerful state, the results of which (it seemed to him) were only too evident in contemporary Nazi Germany and Soviet Russia. By the mid-1940s he had begun a reassessment of his political loyalties that would draw him toward the Liberal party by the late 1950s.

This shift in allegiances brought him notoriety and cost him some of his friends, but the political apostasy masked a good measure of intellectual continuity and consistency. His earliest political memories were Liberal, with a capital "L": a picture of Sir Wilfrid Laurier's first cabinet had hung in the dining room of his family home in Stouffville, Ontario, where the newspaper of choice (and source of the Laurier photograph) had been the Toronto *Globe*, then still the voice of Ontario Liberalism that it had been since the pre-Confederation days of George Brown, its first and most famous editor.[5] Underhill began the leftward journey that would eventually take him to the LSR and CCF when, after graduating from the University of Toronto in 1911 with his BA, he went to Oxford University for further study. There, in what was in many ways the intellectual centre of the British Empire, he was exposed to Fabianism (a gradualist, as opposed to revolutionary, form of socialism) and the New Liberalism (a modification of classical liberal individualism in a collectivist direction). Together, the two sets of ideas laid the foundations of social democracy in the English-speaking world, an approach to politics that combined a belief in the virtues of freedom and tolerance with an equally strong belief that their benefits could only be experienced universally if the state acted to mitigate the effects of social inequality.[6] Underhill's eventual socialism – and that of many others – represented the leftist face of social democracy. Neither Marxist nor communist, it was socialism understood as an advancement on the democratic liberalism of the nineteenth century.

Underhill's turn to Liberalism in later life was thus a return to his roots, but it did not entail a repudiation of the small "l" liberalism to which he had always adhered. It accepted rather the centrist face of social democracy, akin to that represented earlier by Franklin Roosevelt's New Deal in the United States during the 1930s and the passage of unemployment insurance legislation in Canada in 1940, and later by the creation of a national medical insurance plan, Medicare, by the Liberal government of Lester Pearson. Such a plan had, in fact, been one plank of the Regina Manifesto and had first been introduced in the province of Saskatchewan by a CCF government. Pearson had been something of a fellow traveller of the CCF in the thirties, sympathetic to many of its aims, if unpersuaded by its program as a whole, and constrained in expressing his views by his position in the Department of External Affairs. He and Underhill were old friends, in the small world of the English-Canadian political and cultural elite, and Underhill welcomed his election as leader of the Liberal party in 1958, writing to encourage him to open the party to its critics on the left, and to craft a platform that would be liberal with a small "l" (as well as large).[7] It was not a huge leap intellectually to see the Liberals as a potential vehicle of social democratic reform. The party had long harboured others besides Pearson who were "progressive" in their outlook.

Underhill's public life thus offers a window on the intellectual landscape of twentieth-century Canada, both on the role of the intellectual – an entire sensibility as much as a particular manner of political criticism – and on the origins and progress of what might be called the social democratic age in Canadian history, which opened during the Great Depression of the 1930s and continued until the end of the Cold War and the apparent triumph of free market capitalism in the early 1990s. The emergence of the intellectual and the rise of social democracy were landmark events in the history of the twentieth century, even if they require that we expand the meaning of "event" to include the kind of extended period in which intellectual change always occurs.

It is possible that the lives of others might suit the purpose just as well. Frank Scott, for example, Underhill's partner in forming the LSR, was also engaged by issues of academic freedom in the 1930s and 1940s, though the most serious of them involved colleagues rather than himself. He wrote on broad questions of public policy from his perch as a law professor at McGill University, and he made a reputation as a poet that equalled, if it did not actually surpass, his reputation as an intellectual. He was also active in the CCF from its beginnings. Indeed, he remained active in the CCF longer than Underhill, through to its reorganization as the New

Democratic Party in 1961 and beyond, though paradoxically he was more conservative in his socialism than Underhill through the 1930s and into the 1940s. Another possible alternative is A.R.M. Lower (1889–1988). Unlike Scott, who was somewhat Underhill's junior, Lower was exactly his contemporary. A prolific scholar on the history of the timber industry in Canada, Lower wrote widely on just about anything he felt inclined to comment upon, though in the 1930s this meant international affairs and Canada's external relations more than anything else. Never a supporter of the CCF, he was a liberal (and Liberal) nationalist and came to acknowledge the need for a more socially oriented liberalism only later in life.

Underhill, however, is an especially compelling index of change for a number of reasons. For one thing, his own primary intellectual guides were revealing. His student Kenneth McNaught once wrote of him that he had two heroes above all others: one was Woodsworth, the passionate Christian socialist, a "prophet in politics" in the evocative words of the title of McNaught's biography of him, the origins of which, as it happened, lay in a PhD thesis written under Underhill's direction; the other was John Stuart Mill, the nineteenth-century theorist of liberalism, as a philosophy both of individual liberty and of state intervention designed to expand the opportunities for individual self-fulfilment.[8] There were no better models of public engagement and no better touchstones of social democracy. For another thing, Underhill's commitment to a cause – often expressed with a sharpness that aroused irritation among his friends as well as hostility from his enemies – was combined with an acute self-awareness. He was an intellectual, and he thought about what being an intellectual meant; he was a social democrat, but he never stopped thinking about where that might lead him and his comrades-in-arms.

Third, Underhill was a man of restless curiosity, attuned to the broader intellectual currents of his time. No wide-eyed utopian, his belief in human rationality and the potential for social improvement was tempered by service in the First World War

and by a lifetime's reading of skeptics and conservatives, ranging from the seventeenth-century English philosopher Thomas
Hobbes, who held that life in the state of nature was no idyll
but a war of "every man against every man," and whom
Underhill first read as an undergraduate; to the lapsed Fabian
socialist Graham Wallas and the American journalist and mass
media critic Walter Lippmann, whose arguments that people in
the mass were moved more by image and impulse than by
rational thought he read as they first appeared, early in the
twentieth century; and to the mid-twentieth century philosophers of American conservatism Russell Kirk and Peter Viereck.
Underhill never ceased attempting to integrate such contrary
world views into his own thinking. The result was a layered
conception of liberalism and a capacity for detached observation of which we may here be the beneficiaries.

For all of the underlying continuity in Underhill's thought –
perhaps more properly considered his "pre-political" or "sub-
political" attitudes and beliefs, to borrow a term from Stefan
Collini – the positions he adopted on various questions
changed over time, sometimes over a very short period of
time.[9] His move from the CCF to the Liberals was only the
most famous of these. Less well known – though equally
important, as we will see – was the muting of his basic idealism about Canada and Canadian nationalism in the aftermath
of the First World War and his adoption of an attitude of
strict realism about the exercise of political and economic
power by the end of the 1920s, and a resulting skepticism,
sometimes shading into cynicism, about the very idealism that
he himself had espoused not too long before and that continued to underlie his thought and action. He had even expressed
support for the view that Canada would find its place in
world affairs most effectively through its membership in the
British Empire, a position he would shed as his doubts grew

of the capacities of Canada to influence British imperial policy. An internationalist in the 1920s and an isolationist in the 1930s, he became a Cold War liberal in the 1960s; a critic of Roosevelt's New Deal in the thirties, he revised his opinion in retrospect a decade or so later.

The same inconsistency can be observed in more minor spheres of thought and action. When he moved to Saskatoon in 1914, he couldn't believe what a cultural wasteland it was, yet he also took pleasure in noting that the *Manitoba Free Press*, which he first read *en route* to his destination, was a far superior newspaper to any in Toronto. He also attempted to replicate the English habit of tea in the afternoon, in his flat, despite having been put off by his la-di-da English classmates in Oxford. Similarly, when he later found himself in an English county regiment in World War I he felt isolated from his fellow (upper class) officers, but when he returned to the Canadian Corps at the end of the war he lamented the mundane level of conversation in the mess, compared to that he had just left. (He also complained of the absence of afternoon tea.) Back in Saskatoon in the 1920s, he yearned for an appointment at the University of Toronto, but soon after he got one he regretted having left the lively political scene in the West and bemoaned the philistinism of Torontonians.

These sharp swings in mood and outlook continued throughout his life, leading some historians to conclude that he was an unreliable prima donna, aspiring after some goal only to become disenchanted once it was achieved. This is a judgment that may say as much about the expectations of the judge as about the subject. Underhill undoubtedly had a volatile personality. To all appearances cool and rational, and admired by many of his students and colleagues for his clear and logical thinking, he was also a man of enthusiasms, passions, and a good dose of nervous energy, which led him to speak directly, react (and overreact) quickly, and call a spade a spade, as he saw it. He undoubtedly took pleasure in defying conventional wisdom as well, especially when it was expressed by those in positions of power and influence – and, one suspects, when it was clear that they were not as smart as he was. I think it is a mistake, however, to attribute Underhill's inconsistencies to some failure of character.

His changeability needs to be seen, rather, in the context of his unceasing intellectual activity. His mind would not stay still. He read compulsively – always with a pen or pencil in his hand – and wrote incessantly. The most complete bibliography of his work was compiled by a former student, Norman Penlington, who edited a Festschrift published in Underhill's honour in 1971.[10] The festschrift as a whole was oddly unrepresentative of the honoree's former students and colleagues (somewhat to his dismay), but Penlington's painstaking compilation of nearly everything Underhill had written, including numerous items that had appeared anonymously in the *Canadian Forum*, compensated for the book's otherwise uneven quality. Some sixty pages in length, the bibliography listed book reviews, encyclopedia entries, articles published in academic journals, transcripts of radio broadcasts (though many more of these could not be traced), chapters of books, pamphlets, contributions to essay collections, introductions to edited volumes, essays published in general interest periodicals (ranging from the university quarterlies to *Saturday Night*, *Maclean's* magazine, and the daily press), and a prodigious number of occasional pieces that appeared in the *Forum*, signed (famously as "F.H.U.") and unsigned. (It sometimes seemed as if entire issues of the *Forum* must have been written by Underhill.) Close to two thousand separate items were listed.

Unpublished writings were not included. Underhill wrote assessments of book manuscripts for publishers and granting agencies, and was generous in commenting on drafts of work sent to him by colleagues. He wrote speeches that he gave to service clubs, the L S R , Ontario Woodsworth House (the educational centre he helped to found in Woodsworth's memory), student clubs, the Canadian Institute on Economics and Politics (better known as the Couchiching Conference, after its location at Geneva Park on Lake Couchiching), the Canadian Institute of International Affairs, branches of the League of Nations Society, meetings of the CCF (in the 1930s) and the Liberal Party of Canada (in the 1960s), and other groups besides. He also, of course, wrote the lectures he delivered in the normal course of his duties as a university professor.

His published work and his correspondence – I haven't mentioned his voluminous correspondence – reveal a man constantly debating with others, and often with himself, his enthusiasm ever in tension with his skepticism, and his inveterate shyness with his combative audacity. He was not one to hold to the middle way, blamelessly marking time, offending no one (as he once charged his university colleagues of doing). Yet there were no absolutes and few certainties. The context of debate changed, in both the short and the long term, and Underhill responded to new circumstances. This, I think, is the mark of a true intellectual.

It is often said that historians are inevitably influenced in their choice of subject and the approach they take to it by the positions they adopt on the events and issues of their own time. Underhill certainly thought this and did not hesitate to say so, whether in his historical writing or in his commentary on contemporary affairs. In my experience, the influence just as often works in the opposite direction; that is, one's position on current issues is shaped by what one has learned in studying the past. In the present case, my previous work on Charles Clarke, a nineteenth-century Radical journalist, small-town merchant, and politician – and an earlier example of something like an intellectual in Canada – gave me a new appreciation of liberalism in its radical form, especially of its optimism about the possibilities for social improvement in an era when the human potential for self-fulfilment seemed infinite.[11] My study of

Clarke also led me to wonder how it was that radical – or "left" – liberalism shifted ground from its emphasis on localism and small government in his time to centralism and an interventionist state in the twentieth century; that is, how it shifted to social democracy. The answer to this is complex and has been investigated by other historians, but a part of the answer, I realized, might be found in Underhill's biography.[12]

There is another aspect of Underhill's life and thought that might give us reason to pay it some close attention. In a time of social and political change, not to say upheaval – the "roaring twenties" and the "dirty thirties" – he was faced with the challenge not only of communicating what he had learned about the past as a historian, but of disseminating his ideas of what actions ought to be taken in the present. He had to find a medium of communication and a language and style suited to the posture he adopted, and to the arguments he wished to make. He found the first in the small, independent magazine press, particularly in the *Canadian Forum*, which he edited for a short time as well wrote for, and the second in the "discourse" of the intellectual, which he had to invent as he went along. A similar challenge exists today, when the habits of thought, modes of expression, and instruments of reform of the twentieth century seem to have lost the force of persuasion they once had. Social democracy itself has been in retreat for the past twenty years, under attack for both its failures and its successes, and many are searching, as Underhill once did, for a language and tools suited to the needs of our time. Perhaps his example can offer clues – or at least inspiration – that might aid in this search.

I

Satiric Observer

Underhill is still a little clammy and prefers the part of satiric
spectator.

Kenneth N. Bell, 1911

When Underhill went to Balliol College, Oxford, in 1911, he
did so partly on the recommendation, and at the urging,
of G.M. Wrong (1860–1948), the head of the Department of
History at the University of Toronto. Although Wrong was
not (in Underhill's later recollection) among the best, intellectually, of his lecturers and tutors, he paid close attention to
the progress of his students and encouraged the best of them
to pursue further study after completing their undergraduate
degrees. He acted as something of a mentor to Underhill. He
also regarded Oxford as the very model of an ancient university, with the result that he not only steered his best students
there but structured Toronto's own history program and
teaching methods along Oxford lines and, when he could,
hired its graduates to fill positions in the department. The
Balliol imperial historian Kenneth Bell came as a visiting professor in Underhill's final two years, and when he returned
home he kept Wrong apprised of the progress of his stellar
graduates – "your young people" – after they arrived. They
included Charles Norris Cochrane, later an eminent classical
scholar, and Carleton Stanley, who went on to become president of Dalhousie University, as well as Underhill. Cochrane,
according to Bell, was doing the best of the three at first
("beginning to talk excellently"), while Stanley was still rather

"angular and challenging in his attitudes" and Underhill "a little clammy" and aloof. [1] Oxford was the training ground of gentlemen as well as scholars, which was why Wrong had recommended it in the first place. Underhill never fully managed to conform to the standard.

His academic progress, on the other hand, was everything Wrong might have hoped for. In another letter, Bell urged Wrong to send over a woman student he had taught during one of his years in Toronto, a Miss McMurchie, describing her as "a female Underhill" – and, he added, was Underhill not "a Balliol Star of the first magnitude"? He reported that A.D. Lindsay, Underhill's tutor, had told him that the young man was doing "unmistakably 1st class work" and was "a very able man." [2] There was no higher praise in the lexicon of British academic judgment than to be deemed "a very able man," and it showed that Underhill impressed his Oxford professors no less than he had already impressed those at Toronto and his teachers before them at Markham High School.

He grew up, the older of two children, in a comfortable middle-class household. While Stouffville was no industrial Hamilton or Montreal – he was later to recall that he only really became conscious of class in its industrial meaning when he went to England – his father, Richard Underhill, was a small-scale boot-and-shoe manufacturer and a member of the Stouffville governing elite, serving terms as municipal councillor and reeve. When Underhill was still an infant, the family moved from the apartment they occupied above the shoe shop into a substantial three-storey brick house of the kind that still dots the towns and villages of rural Ontario, to the wonderment of present-day weekend travellers unaccustomed to the wealth-generating potential of pre-industrial and early industrial economies. "Respectability," though, as much as wealth, marked the dividing line between families like the Underhills and the labouring and servant classes.

Richard Underhill was also an active Liberal at a time when the party name still carried some of the associations of earlier "Grit" radicalism, and when elections were still regarded by many party loyalists as contests between the forces of light (themselves) and the forces of darkness (their Conservative opponents). The great projects of economic development now mythified as monuments to Sir John A. Macdonald's national vision, like the Canadian Pacific Railway, were seen by Liberals at the time as profligate and corrupt expenditures of public money. (As an undergraduate at the University of Toronto, Underhill was later shocked to hear J.S. Willison, the worldly editor of the *Globe*, describe elections as contests between the "ins" and the "outs.") The Clear Grits of mid-century had been democrats who favoured extension of the franchise, the secret ballot, and representation by population, while believing that social advancement was open to all who worked hard, took advantage of their educational opportunities, and adopted the habits and mores of their respectable superiors. The Underhill family's English forebears, in Frank's later recollection, were political and social cousins of the Ontario Grits, lower-middle-class radicals and reformers disenfranchised in England until the Second Reform Act of 1867. The Underhills, in short, were Liberals not merely by voting habit; though familiar enough with the seamier side of electoral politics, they were liberals in principle.

It was sometimes with complete seriousness, then – if more usually with a touch of self-mockery – that Underhill told audiences in later years that he had been born a "North York Presbyterian Grit." The "North York" qualifier reinforced the radicalism of his Liberal ancestry by evoking the region's reputation as a hotbed of discontent in the Upper Canadian Rebellion of 1837. Another connection with the rebellion that he also took pleasure in noting was his friendship, dating from high school, with Charles Lount, a descendant of Samuel Lount, one of the men hanged for participating in it. The "Presbyterian" part of the description was a nod especially to his mother Sarah. While the entire family regularly went to church, Frank and his younger sister Isa attending Sunday school, Richard Underhill and one or two of his friends expressed an element of skepticism by absenting themselves from communion. Sarah had no such reservations and almost certainly was the one mainly responsible for instilling in the children a Calvinist sense of rectitude. The touch of mockery in Underhill's self-description derived partly from the fact that he gave up his religious beliefs before graduating from university and becoming the "satiric spectator" observed by Kenneth Bell. It was also the product, of course, of his leftward political progress.

Just as important as his social background, if not more so, in shaping his mature outlook, was the era in which he grew up. We will only appreciate Underhill, in fact, in both his consistencies and his inconsistencies – and in his professional practice – if we take into account that he grew to adulthood prior to the First World War. He was twenty-four years old in August 1914, and the end of the war came on the eve of his twenty-ninth birthday. He himself understood this well enough, but whenever he drew attention to it, he did so with enough of a twinkle in his eye to disguise its seriousness. "He or she who was not born soon enough to grow up in that delectable quarter century before 1914," he said on the occasion of his eightieth birthday party, "can never know what the sweetness of life is."[3] One imagines a chuckle rippling through his audience, but it is also hard not to think that beneath the irony lay an experience of the twentieth century – of warfare, depression, and social upheaval; of fascism, communism, and the cult of the masses – as a kind of Fall. "Most history," the American literary critic George Steiner has written, "seems to carry on its back vestiges of paradise," and this would seem to have been true for Underhill.[4] This is not to suggest that the ideas of one's youth determine one's future, any more than do the social circumstances of one's earliest years, but it is often the case that young men and women form an idea of the world and its ways as they come intensively to grasp ideas on

first acquaintance and work out their implications and connections.[5] What was Underhill reading, then, in his teens and
early twenties? What was he thinking about?

Underhill left a record of his intellectual formation in his
undergraduate essays and in later recollections. Among the
latter, the birthday speech referred to above is by far the rich-
est source of information, amounting to a two-hour autobiography: "The Education of Frank Underhill," he called it.
The *Globe*, he told his listeners, was not only the newspaper
to which his family subscribed; so also had his mother's family before them, and he thought that it must have been the
instrument of his own reading education. Sets of books came
into the house by purchase from travelling salesmen, while
magazine subscriptions were bought from boys who sold
them door-to-door, a practice that continued through the
middle years of the twentieth century, as I can personally tes-
tify. In this way, during his high school years Underhill came
to read the American periodical press of the day – *Collier's
Weekly, Harper's Weekly, Scribner's Magazine, The Atlantic
Monthly, McClure's Magazine*, and others. Those that the
family did not purchase could be read at the local library by a
young person as bookish as he evidently was. Especially
memorable were the great muckraking exposés of contemporary American journalism that these magazines carried in
serial form before they were published as books: Ida Tarbell's
History of the Standard Oil Company (1904), Lincoln
Steffens's *The Shame of the Cities* (1904), and Upton Sinclair's
The Jungle (1906).[6] The liberalism of his youth was tinged
with the flavour of American Progressivism and its critique of
unfettered capitalism.

Underhill did not actually read any American history at this
point, but he did read some English history. An aunt gave him
a copy of Charles Dickens's hugely popular *A Child's History
of England*, and in school he read the almost equally popular
A Short History of the English People, by J.R. Green. These
were both books that an earlier generation of "advanced"

liberals had also read, another indication of nineteenth-century continuities. Reading Dickens, he said, immunized him from undue regard for the British monarchy, while the vividness of Green's depiction of individual characters and of the English people acting together – even if the essence of what Herbert Butterfield was to criticize as "the Whig interpretation" – stimulated his interest in English history. Most important for his future, the principal of Markham High School, himself a graduate of the honours classics program at University College, convinced both Underhill and his parents that he ought to follow in the principal's footsteps.

So few young people went on to university in the early twentieth century that it is difficult now to imagine just how exclusive was the club that he was joining. When he graduated from the University of Toronto four years later, in 1911, he was one of a class of only twenty-two students. His standing was high: 1.1 in the English and history program (that is, a first-class mark – an "A" in today's parlance – and first in his class); 1.3 in Classics; 1.2 in both Latin and Greek; and 1.2 in Modern History. His main competitors were Carleton Stanley and Charles Cochrane, except in Modern History, where Mossie Waddington, who remained a friend for the rest of his life, finished 1.1.[7] It was regarded at the time as the finest graduating class in the university's history. Small wonder that Underhill – and Stanley, Cochrane, and Murray Wrong, G.M. Wrong's son (though not Miss Waddington) – went on to Oxford.

In the four years from 1907 to 1911, the wider world opened up to him, and the study of political ideas, in particular, swept him off his feet, to use the phrase that became one of his favourites for describing the impact of particular individuals on his thinking: John Stuart Mill; Ramsay MacDonald, the British Labour party leader; Charles Beard, the American economic historian; and others. Matthew Arnold, the nineteenth-century cultural critic, and John Morley, the longtime editor of the *Fortnightly Review* and right-hand man (and biographer) of

William Ewart Gladstone, the Grand Old Man of English Liberalism, became "heroes" of his, to use another favourite term. The distinctive quality of his undergraduate education was its combination of classical and modern subjects, both approached by reading and writing about the major texts of major authors. This is a method now long out of fashion and followed only in a few "great books" courses, such as in the Foundation Year Program at the University of King's College in Halifax. Its weakness lay in the consideration of texts without much regard for their historical context, which may help to explain why Underhill's later work has been criticized by historians of historical thought. Its strength lay in its attention to close reading and its emphasis on clear and persuasive writing, which was reinforced by the demands elsewhere in his program of mastering Latin and Greek composition.

The essays he retained were doubtless among his best and concerned subjects that continued to hold his interest: Mill, Edmund Burke and Thomas Hobbes, Hobbes and John Milton, Hobbes again (specifically on his *Leviathan*), and William Makepeace Thackeray. The Mill essay won him the English department's Frederick Wyld Prize in his graduating year, worth $75, which he promptly spent on acquiring the complete works of Matthew Arnold and John Morley. He wrote the essay on the *Leviathan* for a third-year English seminar on Milton and his contemporaries offered by Dr Malcolm Wallace, who gave it a mark of 90, commenting drily, "A very interesting and very adequate paper." This may say something about the understatedness of professorial praise at the time. Many years later, Underhill learned from Wallace's daughter, the historian Elizabeth Wallace, that her father had often spoken of the pleasure it had been to have Underhill in his class and to read the kind of essays he wrote.[8]

It is easy to see why, reading them today. Their prose is remarkably clean and uncluttered, their judgments confident. In retrospect, Underhill thought that one advantage of his classical studies had been that, in having to write essays in

Latin and Greek, he had been led self-consciously and purposefully to organize his thoughts and arguments, rather than simply letting them flow naturally, in a "formless kind of prose," as he might have done writing in English, and to express himself concisely. The self-consciousness was evident in his frequent use – even excessive, in the zeal of first discovery – of particular kinds of constructions, notably parallelisms: "Hobbes is the radical philosopher, Burke the conservative," he wrote in concluding an arresting introduction to "Burke and Hobbes as Guides to Modern Democracy"; "Hobbes the skeptic; Burke the mystic. The one wins our admiration for his clearness and consistency in thinking; the other for his depth. We listen to the arguments of one with applause for his brilliance; to those of the other with reverence for his wisdom."[9] The stylistic ease that would later become Underhill's trademark was cultivated from an early age and achieved only after considerable effort and practice.

There was also already apparent the personal voice and direct manner that marked his mature prose. "The 'Leviathan' of Hobbes is, I suppose, one of the greatest books of political philosophy ever written," he began one of the essays he wrote for Wallace. "It is at any rate one of the most delightful."[10] Writing of his appreciation of Burke's *Reflections on the Revolution in France* a year later, he commented, "It would be almost impossible, I should think, for even the most vehement radical to study his works without attaining to a more chastened spirit." The forthright expression of personal judgment is only one way in which his essays differ from those written by university students today, which are expected to suppress personal voice in emulation of the quasi-scientific detachment of the scholarly article. Underhill also drew lessons for the present, rather than confining himself to an analysis of the text in its own time. Thus, he ventured the conclusion that the leader of a modern democracy, tempted simply to follow "the shallow thinking of the masses" for popularity's sake, might find in Hobbes an example of courage in the face of conventional opinion, whatever his view might be of Hobbes's philosophy as a whole. "Against this spirit of intellectual laziness," he went on to say, "the determination of Hobbes to prove all things, his refusal to be guided by accepted opinions unless they can justify themselves before the bar of his reason stand out in admirable relief." This is not the sort of judgment a modern student is invited to make in a term paper. In comparison with these sharp differences in substance, the complete absence of scholarly apparatus in Underhill's essays, which had neither footnotes nor bibliography, seems almost minor.

In short, he wrote essays in the mode initiated by the French humanist Michel de Montaigne four hundred years earlier and carried forward – indeed, brought to a modern flowering – in the periodical journals and magazines that proliferated in the nineteenth century. He was thoroughly familiar with these, not only in the magazines that he read at home, but in essay collections by men such as Leslie Stephen, one of the pre-eminent "men-of-letters" of late Victorian England (and father of the novelist Virginia Woolf). The "thesis/support" form of modern academic scholarship is an altogether different mode of expression and one foreign to Underhill's experience.[11]

Perhaps even more striking to the modern reader is the approach his essays took to their subjects, which was essentially to engage with them in argument. Instead of asking where an idea came from, or how it responded to those put forward by others, or how it found its way into the public sphere, or even what impact it had on contemporary readers, he asked whether it made sense, whether it was consistent with others held by the person (or persons) under study, and whether – as in the case of Hobbes's insistence on rational coherence – it had anything to offer readers in the present. This was explicitly the purpose of his essay comparing Hobbes and Burke and the guidance they might offer to modern democrats, even though neither man was himself a democrat, modern or otherwise. Whether lessons were to be found in their writings, and what they might be, was a matter of judgment, of course, and Underhill did not hesitate to use his.

The exercise of his judgment reveals a young man discovering his vocation. When he read his paper on the *Leviathan* in the Milton seminar, Wallace observed that writing it must have given Underhill great pleasure, and it clearly had.[12] Recalling the experience in his birthday speech sixty years later, Underhill said that in reading the "magic pages" of *Leviathan* it had dawned on him, like a revelation, that "if I was to live a happy life, I must spend the rest of my days studying politics." He had been drawn to Hobbes, he said, as Milton had been drawn to Satan. He could accept neither Hobbes's dismal view of human nature nor the absolute priority he gave to the original contract into which (he argued) human beings had entered as a means of escaping the brutality of their natural existence, yet Underhill admired the rigorous, mathematical logic with which he came to his conclusions, even if the effect was ultimately dogmatic, and he conceded the kernel of truth to be found in Hobbes's rather bleak world view. Hobbes, one imagines, served Underhill as a kind of prophylactic against the utopianism of more optimistic theories of politics and society.

One result, at this stage of his life, was to instill a skeptical view of democracy, which gave the voice of "the people" the absolute sovereignty that Hobbes had accorded the person of the monarch, and to nurture a skepticism likewise of "socialistic democracy," which was apt to forget the truth enunciated by Mill that "the good of society depends ultimately upon the free development allowed to the individual." Socialism placed too high a value on efficiency; that is, on the idea that it was possible to determine the goal to be achieved in solving economic problems and to fix upon the means of reaching it. Underhill was reacting, it seems, to the Saint-Simonian faith in experts and planning that marked contemporary English socialism. "Apparently the more complex that society becomes," he wrote, "the less can the 'laissez faire' policy be justified. But in their zeal for the end they [socialists] forget the men who are to reach the end; their desire for reform leads them to over-estimate measures and under-estimate the gradual education of character which is more important than any measures." This was precisely the failing of Hobbes and the value of turning instead for guidance to Burke, whose cautionary regard for established institutions was based on a sympathetic understanding of human imperfection. Modern democrats might not regret the passing of the aristocracy, but they needed to cultivate a democracy that produced its own leaders, and to ensure that "the people" followed them. The "truest democracy" – and it was a failing of Burke that he did not recognize this – aimed "not at a levelling down to the lowest but at levelling up to the highest; its essential demand is not that the prescriptive privileges of the classes be abolished but that they be shared among all."[13] This was a principle from which Underhill never wavered, and he would often return to the tensions between planning and the contingency of human behaviour.

Nowhere was his engagement with his subject better displayed than in his prize-winning essay on Mill, the initial version of which he wrote for a fourth-year English seminar on nineteenth-century English thought, similar to the one he had taken the previous year on Milton. Reflecting back on it on the occasion of his birthday party, he said that he supposed he had never "got much beyond" Mill's *Essay on Liberty* and "his later socialism." While this may have been true of where his thinking eventually took him, allowing for some rhetorical exaggeration, there is little evidence in the essay itself that Mill's socialism had yet had much influence on him. The essay was rather an examination of the rigorous schooling in utilitarianism – the philosophy that defined what was good in terms of "the greatest happiness of the greatest number" – that Mill had received from his obsessively rationalist father, James Mill, and from Jeremy Bentham, the chief proponent of utilitarianism. It was also an appreciation of how Mill had managed to survive the process with his humanity intact, and to avoid the doctrinaire excesses of his two teachers. Situating Mill, more than his other essay subjects, in the context of contemporary thought – the political economy of Adam Smith and David Ricardo, the positivism of Auguste Comte, as well as utilitarianism and its critics – Underhill concluded that Mill's individualism was tempered by a recognition of social demands arising from altruism and a sense of mutual obligation. Similarly, his adherence to the principle of laissez-faire was qualified by a recognition of the need for "state interference" to remedy pressing social grievances, even if the purpose was "to make further interference unnecessary."

It may be too much to suggest that Underhill identified with his subject in this essay, but it is tempting to see in his admiring introductory characterization of Mill a statement of the ideals that guided his own conduct long afterward: "To be sure," he wrote, after noting that Mill's works had been published in cheap editions and been widely available in England, "he was not afraid to tell the working-classes to their face that they were mostly liars; he always expressed the greatest scorn for English social life; he never hid the fact that his religious beliefs were utterly at variance with those of most of his fellow-countrymen; he was in the habit of dwelling fondly on the epithet he had given the Tories of 'the stupid party'; his radicalism differed largely from that of many who composed the Liberal party, and his support of democracy was always tempered by a very frank confession of its weaknesses and dangers."[14] Nevertheless, Mill's popularity among the English people during his lifetime was virtually universal, a combination of qualities surely worthy of imitation. He embodied in his person the intellectual leadership that ideally an educated populace might follow and embrace, but that was threatened by the "collective mediocrity" to which democracy and the tyranny of the majority were vulnerable. Underhill's response to Mill also made it apparent that the polarities of individualism and collectivism, and laissez-faire and state intervention, are better understood on a spectrum of meaning, more or less prominent according to the needs of the moment, than as fixed abstractions.

———

The following years at Balliol College were in some ways more of the same, except, of course, that it was *Oxford* that Underhill was attending, the centre of his intellectual universe, as it was of many English-speaking Canadians of his generation. For the next decade and a half, and to some extent for the rest of his life, he was haunted by his direct experience of Canada's colonial relationship to the United Kingdom, even after it had ceased to have much political and constitutional significance and had attenuated to a lesser, but nonetheless real, cultural affinity. To the end of his life, he was bound by – one almost wants to say, in thrall to – his regard for Great Britain as a mature society, in comparison with which Canada was, at best, a struggling adolescent. Apart from anything else, when he had criticisms to make of Canadian attitudes, especially toward intellectuals such as himself, it served his purposes to hold up the superior moral position they occupied in the mother country. Long before the end of his life, however, he had freed himself of the deference that characterized official – and elite – opinions of his country's proper relation to the British Empire and Commonwealth, and more particularly to British foreign policy in war and peace. Having regarded the Empire, at first, as the means by which Canada might most effectively achieve some influence in the world, by the end of the 1920s he had come to think of it, instead, as an obstacle to national fulfilment. His ambivalence was partly the product of his upbringing but especially of the years he spent as a student at Balliol and as a soldier on the Western Front during the First World War.

The political and cultural ferment of Oxford in the years prior to the war was exhilarating for a twenty-one-year-old colonial, newly conscious of his intellectual powers and eager for new experiences. Liberal England was entering the throes of its "strange death," in George Dangerfield's evocative phrase, subject to the combined pressures of a rising trade union movement, mounting Irish nationalism, the women's suffrage movement, and the resistance of the House of Lords to the attempt by David Lloyd George, the Liberal Chancellor of the Exchequer, to institute a tax on land.[15] Underhill's professors at Toronto had mainly steered clear of contemporary politics in their lectures. The classicist Maurice Hutton had once observed, as an aside, that "our Canadian history is dull as ditchwater and our politics is full of it," a judgment that Underhill savoured and often subsequently repeated. At the urging of another professor, Edward Kylie, Underhill had met with some Toronto civic reform leaders after he had given a paper on "Commission Government in Cities" to the Historical Club, but this kind of engagement was the exception.[16] Oxford, by contrast, was a crucible of political debate. One could hear speeches by Lloyd George or Ramsay Mac-Donald, read the *Nation* and the *Manchester Guardian*, and join political clubs – the socialist Fabian Society, for example, or the liberal Russell and Palmerston Club. He joined both, an indication of the kinship between them, as well as of their common hostility to the Conservatives.

Politics, it seemed, was everywhere. His tutor, A.D. Lindsay, was an active member of the Oxford Fabian Society, president in the year of Underhill's arrival, and Lindsay's wife, whom Underhill met on Sunday afternoon visits, was a suffragette. The novels of H.G. Wells and the plays of George Bernard Shaw were equal attractions. Both men were prominent social critics, Fabian in their political leanings, though far too independent-minded to stick to any party line. The first of Shaw's plays that Underhill saw in London was *Man and Superman*, which moved and amused him so much that he afterwards took in every one that he could: *Caesar and Cleopatra, Fanny's First Play, Androcles and the Lion, Major*

Barbara, and *Saint Joan*, which he thought the greatest of them all. He admired their satire, wit, and political bite, so much so that Shaw joined Mill and the others in his pantheon of heroes. The playwright, he thought, adroitly combined the roles of humourist and preacher, though as the prefaces to the printed editions of Shaw's plays grew longer and longer, hammering home their lessons, he also came to think that the second role threatened to dominate the first.[17] As in the case of Mill, it is hard not to think that the terms in which Underhill described Shaw – his eye for the sacred cow and his delight in demolishing it, his willingness to take on any subject, his ability to laugh at himself and to bring others to laugh at themselves – represented ideals to which he himself aspired.

His undergraduate education served him well at Oxford. The course of study familiarly known as "Greats" was itself an undergraduate degree, which could be completed in two years by those with a previous degree. He attended lectures and read ancient history and political philosophy under the guidance of his tutor, for whom he produced an essay every week on an assigned topic. The regimen built on the skills he had acquired at Toronto, especially in writing, and he did extremely well, as Lindsay's comment to Bell attests. The tutorial system, Underhill told Wrong several months after arriving, brought the student into close contact with a mind "better trained, clearer, and more experienced" than his own, so attaining something close to the Greek ideal of an education. Many of the tutors were young, lively, and attuned to new ideas and current scholarly controversies (unlike professors at Toronto, he complained), and they were kept on their toes by the high quality of their students and rendered free of the need to teach "third class men" who ought better to have stayed at home (also unlike Toronto). He was conscious of his own conceit in pronouncing on the merits of his alma mater, which, he acknowledged, had awakened him intellectually. Somewhat shy himself, he was irritated and discomfited by the snobbishness and complacency of Oxford students, and by the premium they placed on verbal cleverness and repartee. Nevertheless, the common life of Balliol undergraduates was spent in lively talk on all manner of subjects, again unlike Toronto.[18]

Above all, the difference from Toronto, he thought, was that one's engagement with the classical authors assumed that the questions they dealt with were the same as those of the contemporary world, whether in philosophy or politics. The best students came to realize this on their own at Toronto – evident, as we have seen, in Underhill's own essays – but the classics professors there were more concerned with the grammatical structure of Greek and Latin than with the content of the works they were studying, never mind their relevance in the present. At Balliol, in contrast, students were required in their essays to discuss the pros and cons of issues raised by Plato or Aristotle, and they knew that the same issues, or ones closely related to them, were at stake in debates about the role of the House of Lords in the British constitution, or the taxation policies of Lloyd George. In the terms that he came later to use, Oxford was a school for statesmen, not the training house of academic specialists that many universities were becoming in the United States, and that their Canadian counterparts seemed disposed to imitate.

The resulting mix of interests was evident in the books he bought, taking advantage especially of the riches offered by Blackwell's bookstore, but also of the second-hand book shops of Oxford. Keeping track of his expenses in the Lenten term of 1912, around the time of his letter to Wrong, he listed classical works by Plato, Aristotle, Herodotus, Xenophon, Thucydides, and Plutarch, as well as histories, notably Edward Gibbon's *Decline and Fall of the Roman Empire* and a second-hand edition of Greek historical inscriptions by Edward Lee Hicks, the Anglican bishop of Lincoln and noted clerical exponent of the New Liberalism. More or less equal in number were modern works of philosophy by Hobbes, Hume, Rousseau, Kant, and Mill, including a copy of Karl Marx's

Capital, which he later admitted to finding too impenetrable to finish. He had never bought so many books before. The list also included contemporary works, such as a controversial study of the role of military power in modern international relations by Norman Angell, the Paris editor of the London *Daily Mail* (and emerging pacifist), and a critique of the principle of Irish Home Rule by the most eminent legal scholar of the day, A.V. Dicey, whom he also heard speak in Oxford.[19]

The list is suggestive, rather than conclusive, about Underhill's own evolving political views. On the one hand, it included a study of the workings of the stock exchange by the classical liberal editor of the *Economist*, Francis Wrigley Hirst; on the other, it listed two works by the mid-nineteenth-century philosopher most responsible for dislodging English liberalism from its classical moorings, Thomas Hill Green – his *Prologomena to Ethics* (1883) and his *Lectures on the Principles of Political Obligation* (1895). Another list shows Underhill also reading L.T. Hobhouse's *The Labor Movement* and *Democracy and Reaction*, and he was later to recall that during this period he read Hobhouse's *Liberalism*, which was published in the new Home University Library of Modern Knowledge in 1911 and became a landmark text in defining the New Liberalism. Hobhouse argued that liberalism had grown more socially oriented in the latter part of the nineteenth century, that socialism had grown from the same roots but had moved too far in the direction of a strong state, and that liberals needed to retrieve the democratic spirit of earlier radicals, while replacing their extreme individualism with a vision of an activist and egalitarian state. He emphasized the mutual obligations of individuals in society and the common enemy that all democrats shared in the forces of reaction.[20]

Perhaps of equal interest was Hobhouse's definition of what constituted "reaction," at the centre of which was an aggressively imperialist posture toward Britain's colonial dependencies. He himself had vigorously opposed intervention in the Boer War in South Africa, which had been a defining issue in turn-of-the-century British politics. While support for the war had cut across established party lines – including some somnolent Liberals, he thought, and even Fabians, who became "Imperialists in their sleep" – it came especially from Conservatives, who saw themselves not merely as the defenders of tradition but as proponents of a new, centralized, dominating, militant empire. The costs of the war, the methods used in fighting it, and the injustice of its cause awakened Liberals to the need for "adaptation and growth," while reminding Socialists of the virtues of earlier Liberal principles of "peace and retrenchment." Arguments about the precise limits of liberalism and socialism paled in light of the need to resist the new conservatism; surely, in these circumstances, it mattered little whether one called oneself a liberal socialist or a socialist liberal, a view that drew out the continuities with Mill's liberalism and allayed some of Underhill's earlier suspicions of socialism.[21]

This was the context in which he wrote two essays that survive in his personal papers. Having been invited to join a Fabian research group at Balliol in the 1912–13 academic year, he presented a paper on the history of the trade union movement in England. He traced its roots to the struggle against eighteenth-century laws prohibiting combinations of workers, and he followed its development from the high hopes of Chartism and Robert Owen's Grand National Consolidated Trades Union, through the more narrowly focused organizational drives of the third quarter of the nineteenth century, to its association with the Independent Labour Party in the modern day. More striking than the substance of the paper was its density of detail and its strict chronological ordering of events and institutions; buried in exposition, the argument never quite comes to life. The paper he gave the following year to the Ralegh Club, a new organization formed at the end of 1912 to debate issues related to the British Empire, offered a revealing contrast. In this case, Underhill adopted an explicitly contrarian position, protesting the way in which members of the club seemed to have raised the principle of unity in imperial foreign policy, expressed through a federal organization of the Empire's leading members (meaning the white dominions), to the status of a doctrine.[22]

To begin with, he said, anything doctrinaire inevitably ends up ignoring inconvenient facts and overlooking flesh-and-blood people in pursuit of theoretical consistency, a position he had earlier taken in his criticism of Hobbes. The people who were bound to be overlooked in the pursuit of unity were the inhabitants of the colonies, and the facts likely to be ignored were all of their various interests "summed up in the word nationalism." Warming to his subject, he acknowledged (sarcastically) that mere colonials could not be expected to adopt the "large and generous conception" of the Empire that came naturally to those in the mother country. Nevertheless, the fact that Britain seemed to be able to cooperate with Japan in the Pacific and France in the Mediterranean led one to wonder why a more formal structure was required for men speaking the same language to work together. This was an argument, not in opposition to the Empire as such, but against a centralized conception of its governance.

Adapting the localist sympathies of traditional liberalism, he warned of the defects – the "slackness and inertia" – inherent in central bureaucracies. Finally, apart from the weakness of the argument for unity from a strategic perspective, it seemed to take for granted that the colonies would act irresponsibly if left to their own devices, disregarding the elementary fact of both psychology and politics that an increase in responsibility leads to maturity. There is no evidence to suggest that Underhill took this argument from Hobhouse, but it bore striking similarities to the position taken in *Liberalism*, including a contention that the imperial centralizers tended to be conservatives. Regardless, Underhill clearly had as much fun with "Doctrinaire Imperialism" as he had had writing his paper on the *Leviathan* for Malcolm Wallace's Milton seminar. Imperial relations, and foreign policy in general, were a litmus test of progressive politics and would become Underhill's forte in public debate.

In the late spring of 1913, he completed his degree in *Literae Humaniores* – "Greats" – and learned a few months later that he had achieved a "First." He was offered an assistant lectureship at the University of Manchester to teach ancient history, but he decided against it, at least partly on the advice of Lindsay, who thought he needed a little more maturing before venturing to teach students.[23] The clamminess that Bell had earlier observed had not yet left him. He decided to stay for a third year, studying Modern History, at the end of which he heard from a former classics professor at Toronto, W.S. Milner, that he should accept the offer of a teaching position that he would shortly receive from Walter Murray, the president of the University of Saskatchewan, to whom Milner had recommended him.[24] He was duly appointed (to a full professorship, no less), returning home in time to assume his post in September 1914.

He was in the midst of his homeward sea voyage when war was declared, and from the beginning of his time at Saskatchewan he mulled over the possibility of enlistment in the army. Many of his friends and acquaintances joined up, and there was a widespread feeling, which he shared, that single men his age were duty-bound to serve the Allied cause, and that there was honour in doing so. It may have helped that he found the transition from the sophistication of Oxford and its venerable spires to the frontier town of Saskatoon and its infant university, founded five years earlier, a difficult one. The town shut down completely on Sundays, when everyone, it seemed, went to church. (The fact that he passed on this news to his Presbyterian mother is an indication that his own agnosticism had not caused any serious rift in the family.) What was worse was the thorough-going adoption of co-education at the university. Men and women actually sat together in the dining hall; they also joined each other on the tennis courts, which he thought was probably the reason for the poor quality of play. It was true, he told his mother, that he had a couple of interested women in his classes, but he doubted if their interest went very deep. This was not the last time that Underhill would complain of female students as a category. Also frustrating was the absence of a decent bookstore, which meant that he had to order his books from England and wait six weeks for their arrival.[25]

On the positive side of the ledger, he had been pleasantly surprised to pick up a copy of the *Manitoba Free Press* when his train had stopped overnight in Winnipeg on the way out West. He found it to be "incomparably better" than the Toronto *Globe*. This was the beginning of what he later called an addiction to the *Free Press* and the ideas (and prose) of its long-time editor, John W. Dafoe, though it did not mean by any means that they always agreed. Together, Dafoe and the *Free Press* would make Winnipeg the intellectual capital of Canada in the 1920s, and the prairies the "most internationally-minded and the least parochial" of Canadian regions. Another noteworthy event – literally, one to write home about – was a lecture on immigration that J.S. Woodsworth delivered in January 1915. Afterwards, the two men spoke at some length at a reception held in the president's house. This, too, was a moment of sympathetic recognition with long-term consequences.[26] A final mitigation of his sense of finding himself alone in foreign surroundings was that he began to make friends with a few of his new colleagues. Nevertheless, he continued to feel isolated and also, one suspects, that his talents were being underutilized.

Sometime later in the winter term of 1915, he offered a distillation of his thinking at this point in a lecture entitled "German Political Theory," which took as its subject the political views of the late German nationalist historian Heinrich von Treitschke (1834–1896), and the contemporary military writer and general in the German army, Friedrich von Bernhardi (1849–1930).[27] This required a certain amount of chutzpah. Not only was Canada at war with Germany, but the two men in question were widely regarded as leading proponents of German militarism, especially Bernhardi, whose book *Germany and the Next War*, published in 1911 and translated into English in 1914, had argued that war played a necessary role in the Darwinian struggle for existence, and that nothing limited the German state in the pursuit of its world-power ambitions. Underhill suggested in his lecture that serious-minded people in Canada could learn something from study of the two men's thought.

He began by explaining his choice of subject. "That noble word 'Politics,'" he said, had been debased in North America; Treitschke and Bernhardi, whatever else might be said of them, thought seriously about the nature of the state, of interstate relations, and of the relation of citizen and state, and if their arguments were to be answered, thinking of the same kind was required of their readers and respondents. Little help could be found in the universities, which too often (he said) failed to introduce their students to the great classical texts of political thought – Plato's *Republic*, Aristotle's *Politics*, Thucydides' *History of the Peloponnesian War* – and so to the larger meaning of citizenship. Nor would it come from those commentators who believed that the entire German nation worshipped war and had done so since the Franco-Prussian War of 1870–71. One needed to begin by acknowledging those features that the English and German nations shared in common, such as a commercial spirit. Only in this way would there be a chance of the two acting charitably toward one another when the present conflict ended.

He proceeded to consider the nature and limits of state power, noting in passing the element of idealism in Treitschke's view of the state, whose power was to be enhanced not as an end in itself – the Machiavellian position – but as a means of fostering a national culture. This was a view, Underhill thought, akin to that of many Englishmen in the modern era who favoured the state's assumption of a more positive role than that of the caretaker function contemplated by traditional liberalism. "Some day," he said, "when we in the British Empire come to see the necessity of a greater degree of union among its parts, if it is to be really a state and not merely pious aspiration, we shall be quoting Treitschke as a prophet." A large state, such as the state-like British Empire or the unified Germany that Treitschke had earlier supported, offered greater opportunities for a "rich and noble life" than a small one like Canada, whose politics were "inevitably petty and parochial."

Nevertheless, Treitschke's strong state was more questionable when considered in its international relations. Unconstrained by law or supra-national institutions, the state was free, Treitschke thought, to pursue policy in its own interest, a position taken to an extreme in Bernhardi's exaltation of war as a right and a duty, and his denial of the legitimacy of international treaties. Underhill contrasted this view with that of Norman Angell, whom he had read at Oxford, as we have noted, and who had exposed the "great illusion" of modern times as the idea that war was profitable, or economically advantageous at all, and who had argued that modern developments – primarily economic interdependence (what today we would call globalization) but including the emergence of an international class consciousness – had compromised both the absolute sovereignty of the state and the single-minded allegiance of its citizens. The war might temporarily mean a return to an older and simpler allegiance – and, ironically, to a conception of the state also shared by the enemy – but the restoration of peace would almost certainly mean the restoration of relations cutting across national boundaries, and of Angell's limited state.

Underhill returned to the theme of imperial unity in an essay published in the student newspaper, *The Sheaf*, in March 1915. With the coming of the war, he wrote, it was no longer possible for Canadians to evade their international responsibilities and focus only on their own material well-being, as they had done before. Participation in the war effort as a partner – "on the same basis as England" – brought with it duties and obligations that would not disappear once the war was over. The German threat might disappear, but there would still be "the task of governing the inferior races within the Empire and of lifting them to our own levels of advancement; and that, in the end, will be the greatest contribution which the British empire will have made to the world's history."[28] It would be necessary, that is, to face the question of what "co-operation," that vague word often used in discussions of imperial governance, actually entailed. His support of some greater degree of unity, here and in his Treitschke lecture, was stronger than any he had voiced before, perhaps partly because the idealism he had imbibed in reading T.H. Green and studying with Lindsay was not unlike Treitschke's, and perhaps partly in reaction to the dreary society he had found on his return from Oxford.

Underhill's sense of duty and honour, then, were embedded in an intellectually sophisticated grasp of imperial and Anglo-German relations. During the summer of 1915, when he returned to Toronto for rejuvenation, he made his decision, joining a regiment that promised the opportunity to become a commissioned officer after an appropriate period of training. The news was received with understanding in Saskatchewan, and he was granted leave with half pay, like other faculty and staff who signed up. By the end of November, he embarked from Halifax on the s s *Lapland* for overseas. Months of waiting and seemingly pointless training followed his arrival in England, turning his mood from hopeful idealism to cynical disgruntlement. He appealed to friends at Oxford for help, with the result that he received a commission in July 1916, though in the British army rather than the Canadian Expeditionary Force, which took much of the pleasure from the achievement of his goal. By October he had become a machine gun officer with the rank of second lieutenant in the Hertfordshire Regiment, and a year later he was on his way to France.[29] Frustrating as his two years in England had been, they (and the year before in Saskatoon) had been good for him, he thought; he knew much more of the world and was far more mature than he had been as a callow university graduate.

Underhill's wartime experience was formative in its own way. His letters home focused largely on practical, day-to-day matters, doubtless in part because he wanted both to inform his family of what he was doing and to alleviate their concern for his safety. Occasionally he wrote critically of various military matters – of his gunnery training, which showed a lack of understanding of war as an "applied science"; of French Canadians, for not enlisting in greater numbers – but more often he wrote of his reading, or of the dullness of the routine. He read H.G. Wells's *What Is Coming? A Forecast of Things after the War*, for example, when it came out in 1916, in which Wells anticipated a future United States of Europe, or League of Peace, that would limit national sovereignty in the interests of establishing and maintaining international peace. Underhill liked it so much, he sent a copy to his father.[30]

In March 1917, he noted the general satisfaction derived from news of the revolution in Russia, though this was more in hopes of an improvement in the Russian war effort than a reflection of political opinion, and the following month he described the jubilation felt on hearing of the American declaration of war. When his regiment was sent to France, he assured his father that he was not depressed; on the contrary, this was what he had come for. Over the following weeks and months, he described the fighting he encountered in considerable detail, including the casualties suffered by his battalion and one or two close calls he had himself. In March 1918, in the Battle of St Quentin, he was wounded in his right leg by a machine gun bullet, managed to get to a dressing station, and was sent back to England for treatment, but all this he recounted in the same matter-of-fact manner in which he described everything else.[31]

The diary he had begun to keep in mid-1916 told a rather different story. The entries complained more freely of the

military regimen, and of his social situation. It was impossible
to find time for himself, he wrote, away from his fellow officers and soldiers. This was only partly a lament for the soli-
tude in which he had taken pleasure ever since he had been a
boy with the run of a large house and a nearby public library;
it was also a rebuke of class-conscious English officers, whose
exclusiveness and condescension he resented, much as he had
resented the high and mighty of Balliol, on first encounter.
When he did find time alone, it felt forced upon him by the
same attitudes. The implications were not lost upon him.
Commenting on an article he read in the *Times Literary
Supplement*, he agreed with its observation that the seemingly
minor irritations of social intercourse between colonials and
Englishmen might have unforeseen political effects in the
future. For himself, he found it curious how Canadian he had
come to feel since joining the army, though he could not put
his finger on exactly what it was that made him feel so different. At the same time, his revulsion for the "awful materialism" of Canada – relieved only by a "hopelessly sentimental"
spiritualism – complicated his feelings of alienation.[32]

He encountered the sentimentality of the common soldier
in carrying out the task he was assigned as an officer of cen-
soring letters home. They were full of the "consolations of
religion," which seemed false to him, as did the comfort that
others took in singing hymns at religious services. As a result,
he became increasingly conscious of his own secularism.[33]
Going into battle near Ypres in October 1917, in what became
infamous as the Battle of Passchendaele, it was the battlefield
itself that struck him with awe: "It was a wonderful sight
[that is, it induced wonder] to see the whole landscape a mass
of shell holes and blasted tree trunks." During one stretch of
fierce bombing over several days ("Every evening roughly
from 6–8 we have bomb dropping performance"), of wet
trenches and a shortage of drinking water, he wrote that the
general feeling among his men was of hopelessness, contrary to
the persistent fighting spirit attributed to them by newspaper

correspondents. Everyone, in fact, hoped for peace "with a fervor that would do credit to the wildest pacifist."[34] He admitted to his own fright and discomfort, and felt lucky to have come through the fighting unscathed. Outwardly stoic, Underhill confessed in his diary to drinking more than he had ever done before while on medical leave in the months after receiving his machine gun wound in the spring of 1918.[35] He survived the war skeptical of high-flown talk of sacrifice and noble democratic purpose, especially where it concerned British foreign policy and the rivalries of the European state system.

In the immediate aftermath of the war, on the recommendation of G.M. Wrong, he was recruited by Henry Marshall Tory, the president of the University of Alberta, to teach in the Khaki University, the Canadian YMCA's experiment in providing education – "Rations for the Mind" – to soldiers and veterans overseas. He lectured on British, European, and – for the first time – Canadian history.[36] It was not a bad way to begin the transition to civilian life. When term was over, in June 1919, he headed home after three years in England and western Europe. He never went back.

2

The Past in the Present

The Upper Canada of George Brown and Alexander Mackenzie is our spiritual home; and the struggle from which Confederation resulted ought to have a very special interest to us.

F.H. Underhill, 1927

Underhill returned to the job of a university professor with a feeling of relief. In sharp contrast to the army, here he was in charge of himself (though not entirely, as he was later to discover), and the success of his classes depended on his own efforts. He immediately commenced a regime of constant reading and writing, as if the war had produced an enormous release of energy, rather than the deadening effect that one might have thought natural under the circumstances. On a more mundane level, this was, in part, simply the fulfilment of his professorial duties, which entailed the preparation of numerous lectures, written out virtually in full on long foolscap sheets for formal presentation in class until he grew more comfortable in lecturing and began to use the "talking notes" more common among experienced professors. At first, his courses were all on English and European history, but he was allowed to offer a Canadian course the year after he returned, and at the request of President Murray, he added political science to his teaching load, eventually becoming himself the Department of Political Science. The combination of responsibilities made it possible for him to focus some of his attention on teaching major texts, on the model of his "Greats" program

at Oxford, and as Douglas Francis has suggested in his biography of Underhill, to make Canadian studies an area of concentration to an extent unknown elsewhere in the country.[1]

His rhythm of work was also driven by his desire to communicate what he thought were the lessons of the war. From
the time of his arrival back in Saskatoon, he sought to provide
not only his students but the public at large with the knowledge they required to understand their present world. Early in
January 1920, he delivered a lecture on "The New Europe,"
criticizing the peace settlement emerging at Versailles and
explaining the reasons why Europe had been engulfed by war,
and why, despite the armistice signed in November 1918,
fighting continued in parts of eastern Europe.[2] The fact that
he was in the early stages of mastering his lecturing craft is
indicated by the two notes to himself (charming to any other
practitioner of the craft) at the top of the first page: "1. Ask
questions. 2. Go slow." Early on, he also established his perspective in the drily ironic manner that would become familiar to his listeners over the years. His message would be
recognized, he said, by anyone who kept up with the newspapers, except that in Saskatoon the European news carried by
the local paper, the *Star-Phoenix*, was so mixed up with news
of the hockey team, with Mutt and Jeff (the syndicated car-
toon), and with lists of those who had attended "Mrs. So and
So's dance last night" that it might be missed. He invited his
audience to clear their minds for a moment of all these other
"interesting items."

His explanation of the origins of the war began with geog-
raphy, perhaps in silent tribute to the influence of Sir Halford
Mackinder, whose pioneering work in geopolitics he had read
while a student in Oxford. He showed his audience maps of
the physical features of Europe, of the distribution of its
"races" (ethnic groups classified under the headings of Latin,
Teutonic, Slav, and "Others"), and of the boundaries of its
states, showing how the last of the three seldom coincided with the second. Many countries failed to include all the

people of their major "race," while others included many different peoples. His point was that an understanding of the war began with acknowledgment of the "force of nationality," and that a solution to Europe's historic problems would begin with the implementation of the principle enunciated by US president Woodrow Wilson, and by the Russian Bolsheviks, of the self-determination of nations. The peacemakers' failure to do so completely, and to follow through on the break-up of old empires to their logical conclusion, would condemn Europe to continuing conflict. In listing Switzerland among those states where "racial" and political boundaries coincided, he offered the interesting aside that nationality was not always dependent on "race," and that this was true of Canada as well.

A second criticism he made of the Versailles settlement was of the retribution it proposed to impose on Germany. As he bluntly put it: "A word to those mad men who want Germany to be punished till she can never hold her head up again." The country was now governed by moderate socialists (under the constitution of the Weimar Republic), who were supported by moderates of other parties. What would happen if Germans were driven to extremes? Government would surely fall into the hands of either the "old militarists" on the right or the Bolsheviks on the left. Commenting on the emergence of socialist governments in Germany and elsewhere, Underhill drew his listeners' attention to the "significant fact" that, after four years of war brought on by middle- and upper-class governments, many Europeans seemed to have concluded that socialism was the "hope of the future." While this was hardly a call to arms, it was a sign of his openness to "moderate" socialism.

His reading ranged widely beyond the subjects he was teaching; or, perhaps more accurately, it construed those subjects in the widest possible terms. He became an avid reader of just about everything written by the American journalist Walter Lippmann, whom it is possible he read early in the war when Lippmann first achieved prominence as a "progressive," helping to move liberalism in the United States in much the same direction as it had taken in Britain under the influence of the New Liberalism.[3] Coincidentally an exact contemporary of Underhill's, born in 1889, Lippmann later became disillusioned with democracy and recast the meaning of "public opinion" in a series of trenchant book-length essays. Partly on the basis of his involvement in censorship and propaganda with the American government during the war, and partly grounded in his earlier reading of Sigmund Freud, he became suspicious of the public's capacity for rational judgment and convinced of its vulnerability to manipulation by the clever deployment of images, myths, and symbols. In the conditions of complex modern industrial societies, he argued, people were cut off from direct engagement with their environment; instead, they were caught in a web of perceptions communicated by advertising and the news. It was the responsibility of the rational elite – experts, in Lippmann's terminology – to penetrate beneath appearances and advise decision-makers as to their best course of action.

Somewhat in spite of himself (and perhaps due to his earlier reading), Underhill found Lippmann very persuasive. One of the later books in the series, *The Phantom Public* (1925), was "anti-democratic," he told a correspondent in 1926, but its author was "the most suggestive writer on public affairs in America today."[4] Underhill knew that business and government sought to manage public opinion – to "manufacture consent," in the phrase coined by Lippmann and made current in modern times by Noam Chomsky – by propagating a national interest or ideology, but even as he saw the conservative uses to which Lippmann's analysis could be put, he acknowledged its force. Society and government had become highly complicated, perhaps too much so for the average person to comprehend, requiring specialists to lift the veil of perceptions, interpret complex procedures and operations, and even control them. It was partly in recognition of this that a major theme of Underhill's public

(and academic) commentary became a demand for demysti-
fication and "realism."

Lippmann's analysis was similar to – indeed, was partly
based on – the psychological studies of the early (though subsequently lapsed) Fabian socialist, Graham Wallas. Prompted
in part by popular reaction in England to the Boer War at the
turn of the century, Wallas looked to social psychology for an
explanation of why people acting in the mass so evidently
failed to conform to eighteenth-century Enlightenment ideals
of rational humanity. In *Human Nature in Politics* (1908), he
argued that people arrived at their political opinions not by
rational inference, as many idealistic liberals believed, but
by "unconscious or half-conscious inferences fixed by habit."[5]
By no means cynical, any more than Lippmann was, Wallas
believed that with improved education, better electoral prac-
tices (such as closing public houses on election day), and
"enlightened direction from above," working-class voters
could be led to make informed choices at the ballot box. In a
later book, *The Great Society* (1914), he emphasized that in
the alienating conditions of advanced industrialization, progress would not just happen, nor would it arise from some
transcendent collective will; individual human beings had to
make it happen by means of mundane practical actions.
Underhill read both books in the early months of 1915 and
was later to recall that, together, Wallas and Lippmann had
had the courage to confront the "non-rational, darker sides
of man" and to ask difficult questions about the adequacy of
liberal democratic ideology in the "post-1914 world."[6]

In addition to Lippmann, his American reading in the early
twenties took in the innovative revisionism of the Progressive
historians – Charles Beard, Carl Becker, and Vernon Parrington
– and commentators on the American scene such as the economist Thorstein Veblen, the journalist Herbert Croly, and
the philosopher John Dewey, with the result that he now
increasingly looked southward for new ideas, as well as across
the Atlantic to the Fabians and New Liberals of the United

Kingdom. All of them, though perhaps especially Beard, in his *Economic Interpretation of the Constitution of the United States* (1923), underscored Lippmann's injunction to look beneath the surface of things. At the same time, Underhill was also attracted by the caustic political and social commentary of the essayist and literary critic H.L. Mencken, who assailed the shortsightedness and self-interest of the "booboisie" and the common man alike, and who thereby matched G.B. Shaw as an exemplary disturber of complacency and the status quo. The current of skepticism and realism already evident in the essays Underhill had written as an undergraduate now took on a modernist edge – impelled by what one historian of modernism, Peter Gay, has called the "lure of heresy" – because of both his wartime experience and his voracious postwar reading.[7]

Underhill's first serious venture into historical writing was out of step with his half-formed disposition toward the critical examination of current public issues. It was a study of the Canadian forces in the Great War published in a multivolume history, *The Empire at War*, edited by the imperial historian Sir Charles Lucas under the auspices of the Royal Colonial Institute in London.[8] Underhill's contribution was solicited while he was still at the Khaki University, and he finished it with remarkable efficiency in the following year. Just over 200 pages in length, it amounted to a short book contained within the second volume, along with shorter histories of the war efforts of a dozen other British colonies, including Newfoundland, Bermuda, the colonies of the West Indies, and the Falkland Islands. It was also unusual for him in that military history was hardly his area of expertise. When he completed it in the summer of 1920, he feared that it was "dull" and "too purely military."[9] It might have seemed especially so since Lucas retained strategic and political questions for his own consideration. Still, in the judgment of Tim Cook, the leading modern authority on Canada's role in World War I, it was a "perceptive operational history" and a welcome departure from the memoirs and more superficial journalistic accounts that appeared before it was published in 1923.[10] It was all the more impressive since Underhill had limited access to war records.

Somewhat surprisingly, he later seemed to erase it from his memory, seldom mentioning it or citing it. Perhaps he felt slightly embarrassed at having begun his serious writing life in "imperial military history," as his younger colleague Richard Preston later suggested.[11] Or perhaps, putting this slightly differently, he became embarrassed by the nationalistic judgments that punctuated his otherwise sober and careful descriptions of the fighting in which Canadian soldiers engaged – their "brilliant share" in the Battle of Arras in the spring of 1917, for example, which included the taking of Vimy Ridge; or their "fighting spirit" in face of the "indescribable horrors" of the Ypres Salient, where he also had been, later that same year. Perhaps he shared his professional colleagues' general wariness of operational military history, whatever other differences he had with them. In any case, the conclusion of Underhill's account left no doubt about what he thought in 1920. The Canadian Corps, he wrote, "is the greatest national achievement of the Canadian people since the Dominion came into being; and its story is to be cherished not only as proof of Canadian military capacity but as the noblest example yet given of the ability of Canadians, working in concert with a single inspiration, to accomplish great ends."[12] Whether it was possible for the postwar generation to measure up to such a standard may be doubted, but Underhill's history of the Canadian role in the war is one indication among many of the interest taken by men and women of his generation in their country's national evolution and, more particularly, of their belief that the performance of their citizen soldiers in Europe was testimony to "Canada's entrance into nationhood." The war became central to their sense of identity.

The tensions in Underhill's mind between his hopes for Canada's future and his disdain for the materialism of Canadian life, and between his own earnest idealism and his admiration for the "smartness" of men like Mencken and the realism of men like Beard were evident as he searched for a coherent view of contemporary history in a series of public speeches in the mid-1920s. The main themes that he sought to integrate – Canada's position in the British Empire, its relation to the United States and the wider world, and its debt to those who had fought in the war – were all present in a talk he gave at the University of Alberta in March 1924. One of his duties, he said, as that year's exchange lecturer from Saskatchewan, was to deliver a sermon on a subject of his choosing. His choice, dry though it might be (here he injected Maurice Hutton's dictum on the dullness of Canadian history and politics), was the effect of the recent war on Canada's external relations. He began by reminding his audience of the nation's pre-1914 innocence, what he called its "antediluvian" era. Suddenly thrust into a war not of their own making, Canadians had been confronted by demands that made earlier debates about their role in the Empire academic. In successfully meeting them, everyone seemed to think that Canada had grown into a nation. Shifting from his earlier position, he was not so sure – a skepticism, he said, that made anyone who expressed it "as popular as a modernist in a convention of fundamentalists." Nevertheless, he thought that Canada's participation in the Imperial War Cabinet (giving it a share in decision-making) and its separate representation later in the League of Nations (giving it an independent voice in deliberations) pulled the country's imperial relationship in opposite directions, and no one knew how to resolve the tension.

Those who in more recent times have sought to accommodate the concept of a sovereign Quebec in an independent Canada might sympathize with the challenge presented by the idea of an autonomous Canada in a unified Empire. The corollary, in any event, of a national future defined in some basic way by the imperial relationship was that Canada's relation to the United States was secondary. What, after all, had Canadian soldiers fought for? The answer to that question, Underhill thought, was becoming more elusive as time went on, "but certainly they had not dedicated themselves to the proposition that we are American, that in North America is all our world."[13] Yet, in another speech he delivered at Alberta, he also spoke of America in the first person plural – "our American universities" – as we will see in a moment.

He presented the question of Canada's future rather more bitterly in an Armistice Day address in 1925. The "professional moralists" of 1914, he said, had claimed that Canadians would be refined and hardened into steel in the furnace of war, but their metaphor had distracted them from the "hard facts": "A people cannot give themselves up to a four years' orgy of hating and killing and destroying and expect to have much that is fine or noble or heroic left at the end." Taking stock now, he was even more unsure of what it was that Canadians had died for in the war. Were they any different now than they had been in the "antediluvian" pre-war period? Rather than assuming a greater role in the Empire, or in the world, that might befit their supposedly mature status, they had slipped back into "the old negative isolationist attitude" of 1914, semiconsciously in the grip of outside forces. They might occasionally be persuaded to act the part of Good Samaritan, when what was actually required in the conditions left by the war was a police force to keep the peace. They could not return to their pre-war fixation on buying and selling real estate: "It was not qualities such as these which made the Canadian Corps what it was – the greatest achievement of the Canadian people since Confederation."[14] Underhill's disenchantment with the achievements of the war seemed, if anything, to grow with time. If Canada was indeed a nation, it was not yet clear to him how its new status ought to manifest itself in its external posture.

At the same time, he was also exploring the country's domestic political history, where similar tensions arose. Almost certainly moved by his increasing responsibilities in political science at Saskatchewan, and also by a desire to build a publication record (that might get him to Toronto), he began to investigate the history of Canadian political parties and, more particularly, the liberalism of George Brown, the editor, as we have noted, of the Toronto *Globe* around the time of Confederation and leader of the Réform party. Some evidence of his motivation can be found in the second speech he gave at Alberta, this time mainly to students. His theme here was "political education" and his target, not for the first time, was the deficiencies of "our American universities" in training their students for citizenship. The problem, he thought, lay partly in the primacy accorded the natural sciences in university curricula and the superstitious reverence in which they were held by the public at large. While the sciences had contributed enormously to the advancement of human knowledge, scientific thinking was too narrow for comprehending human society: "Science and the industrial revolution have unified the world so that a shot fired in an obscure Bosnian town costs the lives of thousands of young western Canadians. How are we going to face this new situation and to master it for human good? That is the supreme problem of our generation and it is a political problem."

To make matters worse, the disciplines of the humanities, which might offer some clues to a solution of the problem, were beginning to adopt the research model of the sciences. Instead of joining private observers, practising politicians, and others in writing for "the general cultivated reader" in journals like the *Edinburgh Review*, as was common in England, university professors in America (Canada implicitly included) were increasingly focusing their efforts on journals that were clearly – it was "only too pathetically evident" – written by PhD's for PhD's. Underhill's alternative model was Oxford and Cambridge, which were "schools of statesmen," not PhDs, and which, through programs such as "Greats," educated their students in subjects as a whole, under the primary guidance of one professor, instead of breaking them up mechanically into bits – "courses" – as though universities were factories. North American universities produced graduates unable to understand their large, complex democracies, and unprepared to offer intellectual leadership to their fellow citizens. "The greatest need of our time," he said, "is political thinking."[15] How to meet that need was a matter not only of what was taught, but how it was taught and how it was communicated.

When he searched for a "usable past" (to use the language of later, similarly inclined critics of historical practice), it was natural for Underhill to be drawn to the politics of Canada in an earlier era, and to relate what he found to the politics of his own time, so that the two became inextricably entwined. He began by questioning the conventional wisdom that the two major Canadian parties, Liberal and Conservative, were more or less clones of their British ancestors, Whig and Tory, as they themselves had evolved into Liberal and Conservative. There might have been some truth to this in the period before Confederation, he thought, and especially before the coming of responsible government in the late 1840s, but after Confederation the Liberals and Conservatives lost any affinity they might previously have had with the principles of their namesakes in the mother country and were divided over purely material issues of national development and expansion. This was an idea he was later to turn into a more fully developed interpretation of Canadian party history, but at this early stage of his thinking it helps to answer one of the questions we began with: how the localism of nineteenth-century radical liberalism was transformed into the centralism of its twentieth-century descendant.

For all of John A. Macdonald's unscrupulousness as a politician, in Underhill's telling, he was nevertheless a man of imagination, "seized with the conception of a great Canadian nation." It was he and his Conservative party that absorbed the lands of the Hudson's Bay Company, built the Canadian Pacific Railway, and introduced the National Policy of protective tariffs that stimulated industrial development. In opposition, the one man who might have offered a competing national vision, George Brown, had been followed as Liberal leader by Alexander Mackenzie, a "Scotch peasant" without imagination, then by Edward Blake, who was a great lawyer but an "analytical hair-splitting critical intellectual" and no match for John A. The Liberals only abandoned their "locally-minded," critical, and negative stance – so much for early Clear Grit radicalism – under the leadership of Wilfrid Laurier, when they adopted the nation-building strategies of Macdonald (and his unscrupulousness) and succeeded in winning power. In this way, the two parties became as alike as two Ford cars, the one differing from the other only in being more mud-spattered for having been in, rather than out, of office, which brought Underhill down to the present day, when a new party, the Progressives, had arisen to challenge the old parties and the two-party system itself. Divided internally, they were uncertain how to proceed. In Underhill's view, they had to confront the "real problem," which was how Canada's political democracy was to combat "the monied interests" and control "modern large-scale business and finance."[16] This was the unfinished business of nation-building, and only a period of muckraking such as that which had occurred in the United States two decades earlier – the years of Ida Tarbell, Lincoln Steffens, and Upton Sinclair – would make it possible for a "real liberal party" to form.

The idea that progressive reform was a national, and not a local, undertaking thus took root in Underhill's mind, aided by the national value and meaning of the war effort, and by the example of American progressives to the south. One of the obstacles to the success of a "real liberal party," however, was the absence of anything like a liberal tradition in Canada, and it was in hopes of explaining – or remedying – this that he turned his attention to George Brown. Beginning in 1924

and becoming the focus of concentrated work during a sabbatical leave spent in Toronto and Ottawa in the winter of
1926 and the following summer, he systematically read through
the *Globe* of the late 1850s and early 1860s, classifying and
analyzing the positions it took on the questions of the day.[17]
What he found surpassed his expectations. Instead of railing
against the evils of Roman Catholicism, as the received view
of Brown would have suggested, or obsessing about the minu-
tiae of party manoeuvring, *à la* the Hutton Ditchwater
Dictum, the newspaper attacked the corrupting influence of
business on politics, especially that of the Montreal-based
Grand Trunk Railway, extolled the virtues of the yeoman
farmer standing foursquare on the soil, and called for the
opening of the North West to settlement. In fact, Underhill
found that the political deadlock of the 1860s that gave rise
to the Great Coalition, initiated by Brown, and then to Confederation, was less the result of division between Protestants
and Catholics or French and English, than of the struggle of
an agricultural "West" (Upper Canada) against an industrial-
izing "East" (Lower Canada).

It was no accident that this alignment of forces had a familiar ring. While in Ottawa working in the archives, he was
distracted for a time by debates in the House of Commons
over the customs scandal that brought down the government
of William Lyon Mackenzie King and led to the King-Byng
Crisis. Hours spent in the Visitors' Gallery in June 1926 – and
in J.S. Woodsworth's office, discussing ideas, strategies, and
tactics – reinforced the demands of the present. Underhill had
already come out publicly in Saskatoon in support of the
Progressives, during the election of the previous year, arguing
that the Liberal party offered no hope to genuine liberals.
This was a position later described by the historian of the
Progressive party, W.L. Morton, and by the political scientist
David Laycock after him, as "crypto-Liberal populism," but
Underhill was already moving in a more radical direction.[18]
The example he offered his audience as worthy of emulation

was the British Labour party, whose trade union base, he thought, was analogous in its economic ideas, and in its potential to offer disciplined leadership, to the wheat pools and co-operatives of the farmers' movement.[19] Woodsworth and the "Ginger Group" that he led represented the radical promise of the Progressive movement, and Underhill found in George Brown what he thought was a predecessor and a basis for the tradition he was looking for.

He presented his findings in his first academic paper, written for the 1927 meeting of the Canadian Historical Association (CHA), held in Toronto. Entitled "Some Aspects of Upper Canadian Radical Opinion in the Decade before Confederation," it was one of a half-dozen papers marking the nation's Diamond Jubilee.[20] It is impossible, reading it today, not to be caught up in its overflowing energy, even if one thinks that Brown was not quite as radical as Underhill thought him to be, and that the Clear Grit movement had a more radical phase before it was absorbed into the Brownite Reform party of the late 1850s. A large part of the paper's excitement lay in the context he established at the beginning, the implications and impact of which went far beyond the modest boundaries of his title. If we are to understand ourselves as a people, he wrote, we need to study the social, economic, and intellectual "atmosphere" of a time – the ideas "floating in the air" and the "underlying conditions which made these ideas prevalent" – instead of the biographies of leading men, which only gives rise to hero worship. This was an approach based on his reading of the American Progressive historians, and perhaps of John Dewey's pragmatism as well. He also suggested that the *Globe* and the "'Clear Grit' party" needed to be seen as representing the farmers of the Upper Canadian frontier and therefore as an instance in Canada of Frederick Jackson Turner's "frontier thesis" in operation, the idea that American democracy was the product of the westward-moving frontier of trade and settlement. Underhill was not alone in thinking along these lines – Reginald

Trotter offered a more expressly economic interpretation of Confederation at the same CHA meeting, and W.N. Sage presented an overview of the moving Canadian frontier the year after – but he changed the way Canadian historians approached political history.[21]

More immediately arresting was the direct line he drew from the politics of the mid-nineteenth century to the politics of the present day. Whatever Brown's other achievements, he had failed to lead his fellow citizens into the promised land; instead, the "corruptionists" returned to power after Confederation, Ontario underwent an industrial transformation, and its capital became a "fat and prosperous" city. "No good Torontonian of the present generation," Underhill wrote, prodding his staid contemporaries as usual, "could possibly read Brown's *Globe* without shuddering." It was nevertheless the case that the Clear Grit movement was experiencing a reincarnation on the banks of the Red and Saskatchewan rivers, where farmers were reviving many of the ideas of their Upper Canadian ancestors, even if they did not realize it. "We of the modern West," he concluded, "have a natural affinity" with George Brown's Upper Canada: "It is our spiritual home."[22] Startling as this idea might seem to a twenty-first century reader, especially in western Canada, it resonated in the 1920s, a mere two generations after Confederation. It was the kind of presentist message that Underhill would often repeat throughout his professional career.

The Diamond Jubilee provided him an opportunity to sum up his thinking on Canadian nationhood, past and present, in two speeches he made in Saskatoon. In part, he offered his listeners a popular version of his paper for the CHA. If only Canadians would turn their attention away from the politicians to the real makers of Canada – the farmers, merchants, and lumbermen; the shipowners, railway builders, and bankers; and the preachers, teachers, and newspapermen – they would no longer complain of the dullness of their history but would see its excitement and relevance. More particularly,

they would see that the "essential cleavage" in Canadian politics had always been what it was in their own day, between
Big Business and the little man, between East and West, and
between the constraints of plutocracy and the possibilities
of democracy.[23]

He also asked, as befit the occasion, why it was that Canada
should exist at all. When the nation was formed, hardly anyone
had noticed – German unification having been a contemporary
national birth of much greater moment – and Canadians themselves had shown little enthusiasm for the event then or since.
Perhaps their lack of interest was not surprising, he said, in
view of the fact that their nearest neighbour, the United States,
had been borne in an upsurge of historic vision, high principle,
and creative statesmanship with which Confederation paled in
comparison. What, then, was special about Canada and what
kind of future might Canadians make for themselves? Underhill's answer was that Canadians had been engaged in their
own unique experiment, largely unnoticed by themselves: a
nation comprising "two separate races with different languages
and religions," aspiring to be a part of a larger community, the
British Empire, "independent and yet not quite independent,"
and sharing a continent with a "bigger and more advanced
nation" so similar in its character as to exercise a magnetic
influence on Canadian life.

In describing the first of these defining features, he showed
himself to be a true "North York Presbyterian Grit," calling
attention to the peculiarity, at the time of Confederation, of
the English majority of the province of Canada falling under
the domination of the French minority, and arguing that a
constant challenge of Canadian politics ever since had been
the "perpetual veto" that French Canadians exercised in
national affairs. An obstacle to unity on its own, it also served
to enhance the control of capitalist Montreal. In imperial
relations, the blindness of the English to the national character of their overseas colonies was only matched by the failure
of Canadians to develop a national consciousness, while

– betraying his continuing imperial feeling – a self-centred nationalism of the kind advocated by John W. Dafoe and practised by Mackenzie King would stifle the possibility of the Empire serving as an example to the world in the conduct of international affairs. As if these challenges were not enough, Canadians were burdened by their ambivalent attitude toward the United States, at once admiring and defensive. They had originally come together as a nation, at least in part, in defiance of the American "menace," yet they enjoyed American movies, chewed American gum, spoke American slang, and, if they could afford it, emigrated to California to die in comfort. There was no denying that an American social, cultural, and economic "invasion" threatened Canadian independence.

Underhill's conclusion to all this was to urge his listeners to "face facts realistically": however strongly they might defend their "collective Canadianism," as individuals they were North Americans, for whom the international boundary was actually a bit of a nuisance. The question was, where did that leave those Canadians – among whom he included himself – who believed there was something worth preserving in their nationality? Protection was no answer, in trade or otherwise, not only because it nourished an imitative mediocrity, but because it begged the question of what it was they were trying to protect: "If we want the word Canadian to mean anything we must try to work out a different kind of social organization than the American, not merely a smaller copy of it." There were promising signs of something different from American "individualistic capitalism" in public enterprises like the Hydro-Electric Power Commission of Ontario, the Canadian National Railways, and the Wheat Pools of the prairie provinces. The real hope for maintaining an "independent Canadian individuality" lay in developing "a co-operative commonwealth in the northern half of North America."[24] University activists of the 1960s generation, reading this, might be forgiven for thinking they had been caught in a time warp and transported to a discussion of The National Question

in their own time, yet Underhill was, instead, a slowly blos-
soming social democrat seeking to communicate, in *his* time,
what he believed were hard truths in a new idiom.

————————

Underhill had not actually attended the CHA meeting in
1927, and his paper had been read in his absence by his friend
Charles Cochrane. He had been unable to go, because he had
been busy packing. Earlier in the year, G.M. Wrong had written to say that he was retiring, and a couple of months later
Underhill received an offer of appointment from University of
Toronto president Robert A. Falconer.[25] He considered the
move carefully, but there was little doubt that he would accept
the offer when it arrived. However much he disliked the city
– stuffy, provincial, moralistic Old Toronto – it was home,
and the university a prestigious institution and his alma mater
besides. Five years earlier he had married a colleague in the
English department at Saskatchewan, Ruth Carr, who had
also been a former student of his before the war and had gone
on to do an MA at Toronto. His marriage, and the birth of a
daughter two years later, had given him a new sense of stability and security, which the move to Toronto only confirmed.

Characteristically, he began almost immediately to question
his new circumstances. The history curriculum was too conservative, he thought. It was obviously the product of an earlier era, focused on Great Britain and Europe, when a more
up-to-date program, better attuned to the realities of the time,
would give Canada and the United States the prominence
they deserved. His criticisms, not surprisingly, ruffled a few
feathers, while also showing the continuing shift of his
intellectual focus toward North America. The department he
joined was changing, nevertheless, in ways that reflected
wider changes in the discipline. More emphasis was being
placed on research – a weakness of Underhill's, in the view of
one or two of his new colleagues who had questioned his

appointment, and the subject of earlier letters of encouragement from Wrong – and teaching responsibilities increasingly were assigned in a faculty member's own area of expertise.[26] The immediate impact of these changes is not to be exaggerated, since they would continue to draw comment from critics and defenders alike for another half-century, and one's reaction to them defined one's sense of professional identity.

This was certainly the case with Underhill. In some ways, he welcomed the new regime. In 1926, during his sabbatical leave in Ottawa, he had attended his first meeting of the fledgling CHA, founded only four years earlier, and had been elected to its governing council. He had been especially taken by the possibilities it offered for meeting and socializing with colleagues, and he hoped it would develop on the model of the older American Historical Association. He was the one, in fact, who suggested in 1927 that annual meetings be organized around a particular theme, such as the Diamond Jubilee, and that a lunch or dinner be held to provide an opportunity for friendly, informal conversation. (The economist Harold Innis later reported that the papers presented had varied in quality, but that the banquet at Hart House had been excellent.[27]) The CHA was both an index and an agent of professionalization, encouraging the presentation of scholarly papers and the cultivation of fellowship among otherwise widely scattered members. Periodic trips to the archives in Ottawa served the same purpose, as Underhill had also discovered in 1926. The small community of academic historians – some thirty-five to forty in all of English-speaking Canada – offered him one set of associations, in addition to his family, that relieved the isolation that inevitably accompanied a writing life.[28]

He had also made a point of requiring his students at Saskatchewan to use original sources in researching their essays, and to cite them properly, an injunction that was not unique to the new professionals but one that they increasingly made their own. "In any University history class nowadays," he had told President Murray, "stress is always put on the reading of original documents just as Science class stresses laboratory work."[29] At the same time, as we have seen, he was suspicious of the new status accorded the PhD, and the tendency to specialization and a worship of objectivity that often came with it. He was not about to relinquish his moral judgment, on either historical or contemporary issues, in favour of some protective cloak of neutrality. Speaking to an audience of Montrealers in 1928 on the subject of the historic competition between their city and his own, he suggested that modern Toronto retained the righteousness of the giant-killer it once had been, even though it had become one of the giants itself. "But here I have got down to contemporary politics," he interjected sarcastically, "and as a professor of history I am forbidden to have any opinions about contemporary matters of controversy."[30] Though he embraced the new professionalism, he refused to be defined by it.

The history department was also changing in its personnel. Among his younger colleagues was Lester Pearson, who had joined the department in 1923 but would shortly leave to take up a position in the Department of External Affairs in Ottawa, in part because the demands of research did not excite his interest. Donald Creighton was appointed in 1927, while Edgar McInnis would come in the following year and Chester Martin the year after that. One thing they all shared in common was an Oxford B A, long a qualification favoured by Wrong, though even that was beginning to change. Two years earlier, in 1925, the department had hired George W. Brown, its first member to be appointed with a PhD (and an American one at that). Except for Martin, they were all younger than Underhill and, again except for Martin, who had spent twenty years at the University of Manitoba, all were fresh from their studies, or nearly so, and were appointed at the rank of lecturer.[31] Underhill's own rank remained that of full professor, as it had been at Saskatchewan, though his salary fell by $200 to $4,500, still quite a respectable income in 1927. Over time, his senior rank was sometimes resented by those of his junior colleagues, like Creighton, whose amount of published scholarship, in the form of books and articles, exceeded his own.

Underhill found a different outlet for his energies. Soon after his arrival in Toronto, he began writing book reviews for the *Canadian Forum*, a journal that had been launched in 1920 by a group of University of Toronto professors. Here was another set of associations, even more congenial than his fellow historians, and a publishing venue similar to the British and American intellectual periodicals he so admired. The editors had announced in the inaugural issue that their intention was to provide "a freer and more informed discussion of public questions" and a "distinctively Canadian" treatment of the arts. "Real independence," they wrote, "is a spiritual thing": "No country has reached its full stature which makes its goods at home, but not its faith and its philosophy."[32] The *Forum* focused on Canadian subjects but was also open to ideas from elsewhere and their domestication as occasion required. This was apparent in the journal's format and the impact its editors hoped to achieve – the English *New Statesman* and the American *Nation* and *New Republic* were models they hoped to emulate – as well as in the writing it published.[33]

At first, criticism of drama, literature, and painting – notably the work of the Group of Seven – had predominated, along with original poetry and short stories, and the journal became an influential vehicle of nationalism – though not of the sentimental kind represented by the Canadian Authors Association – and modernism. The literary critic Northrop Frye, writing on the occasion of the journal's fiftieth anniversary, called it "a by-product of a cultural exhilaration that hit Toronto in particular during the early twenties."[34] The city was not so stuffy and provincial, after all, though one would never know it from Underhill's own comments. By the end of the decade, in any case, subscriptions had increased in number from thirty-five – the grand total inherited from *The Rebel*, the student magazine that was the *Forum*'s predecessor – to almost two thousand.[35]

Politics occupied more space as the decade progressed and moved leftward from the liberalism of C.B. Sissons, a classicist from Victoria College who acted as political editor until 1924, to the socialism of J. Francis White, a nonacademic Marxist who joined the editorial board in 1925 and became the journal's first full-time editor in 1927, when J.M. Dent and Sons became its publisher.[36] Underhill's recruitment helped on both counts, though neither he nor most other contributors were Marxists themselves. His style also fit right into the sprightly, humorous tone that had been the rule from the beginning, and his outlook, like that of the journal as a whole, was resolutely anti-romantic. The first book he reviewed, as it happened, was written by one of his new colleagues, W. Stewart Wallace, the university librarian and a member of the history department. Underhill judged Wallace's book, *The Growth of Canadian National Feeling*, a thoroughly competent study, though perhaps overly enamoured of politicians and their influence: "Our politicians," Underhill wrote, "have been the Chanticleers of Canadian nationalism; Mr. Wallace tends to treat them as if they really did make the sun rise."[37] Small wonder that the editors wanted him back for more.

He was soon invited to become a member of the editorial committee, and in 1929 he began writing his own column, O Canada, which made his name as a political and social critic, and established the initials with which he closed every column – F.H.U. – as a mark of intellectual vitality and authority. He began receiving encouraging compliments from readers he hardly knew, like Fred Landon, the University of Western Ontario historian ("I have read your Forum article and think I agree with every word of it") and R.A. MacKay, the Dalhousie political scientist (who enjoyed his column "immensely"), and from men he held in high regard, like Woodsworth ("My only criticism would be that you must not become too pessimistic") and Dafoe ("I continue to read with a considerable measure of joy your contributions to the Canadian Forum").[38] Within a year he was writing two or three reviews as well as his own column for every issue. Toward the end of 1930, he became one of the journal's associate editors, with the result that he began contributing unsigned editorial pieces in addition to everything else. The termination of his personal column in October 1932 did not diminish the quantity or volume of his contributions.

Underhill took advantage of the freedom offered by his O Canada column to take up just about any subject that interested him – politics, business, politics *and* business, the constitution, electoral reform, university education, international affairs, imperial relations, and, as he put it in one column, "the meaning of Canadian life."[39] He also used it to review books on these subjects, frequently quoting passages that he obviously savoured and knew his readers would enjoy. On one occasion, reviewing three books, one of them by the leader of the Socialist Party of America, Norman Thomas, he began by quoting the author to the effect that, twenty years earlier, many people had liked to say, "This is the best of all possible worlds," emphasizing *best*. "Now," Thomas continued, "they say the same words but they emphasize *possible*."[40] Fond himself of the epigrammatic turn of phrase, Underhill appreciated its use by others.

For all of the variety of topics he touched upon, certain familiar themes stand out, among them Canada's international role and what he saw as a growing tension between the demands and possibilities of membership in the Empire – sometimes conceived of more narrowly as the Commonwealth, the term that had come into increasing use since the Imperial War Conference of 1917, denoting Britain and the "Dominions" – and those of membership in the League of Nations. Underhill's devotion to the League had been evident in Saskatoon, when he had begun a League of Nations Club at the university, and when, in 1925, he had written a series of articles for a magazine aimed at school teachers. The League, he wrote, introducing the series, had been created in the immediate aftermath of the catastrophe of the war, in 1919, when "for a moment ... the whole world had a vision of the ideal of the brotherhood of man."[41] It had sought to remedy the two major historic obstacles to peace: the absence of a mechanism to solve international disputes, short of war, and the resort to armaments and alliances as means of ensuring national security. He described the League's constitution, the methods by which it proposed to mediate disputes (including the permanent international court it had helped to create), the system of colonial "mandates" it administered, and – showing that there was more to the maintenance of peace than conventional diplomacy – one of the League's major allied bodies, the International Labor Organization. The League's success, he concluded, depended on the interest that citizens of its member states took in its activities, and the pressure they brought to bear on their governments to support the principle of collective security.[42] Stimulating that interest and pressure was the end he was trying to serve.

The tension between commitments to the Empire and the League showed up more than once in O Canada. Reviewing a study of Canada's role in the modern evolution of imperial diplomacy in 1930, Underhill took the author to task for treating colonial nationalists as too parochial. In fact, he wrote, the only newspaper in Canada that seriously reported on the rest of the Empire was the nationalist *Manitoba Free Press*. To anyone who also read Underhill's academic work, the evocation of George Brown's *Globe* of the 1860s was unmistakable. The year before, he had published an article in the *Canadian Historical Review* on the *Globe*'s view of the Empire, in which he had shown how carefully the paper followed parliamentary debates in the British House of Commons and colonial commentary in the English press – providing lengthy extracts from both for the benefit of its readers – and how it embraced the imperial idea, yet how vigorously it defended Canadian interests and aspirations at the same time.[43] John W. Dafoe was a modern descendant of Brown, for whom nationalism did not preclude close interest in imperial and international affairs; for whom, that is, autonomy and Empire were still reconcilable.

Underhill also made it clear, however, in his O Canada column that imperial cooperation would only be acceptable to the Dominions if it were not regarded as an exclusive loyalty, but instead allowed for attachment to other forms of international association. This was especially important if the Empire were to claim a role in the maintenance of peace: "Most of the orators whose eloquence is aroused by this topic, while they talk about Pax Britannica, are really thinking, as their whole attitude shows, about Rule Britannia." Cooperation, that is, would only be possible if its promoters were also committed to the principles of the League. His pessimism on this score grew with successive examples of the British government acting on behalf of the Empire in international negotiations without consulting the Dominions. The group of people who most needed reminding that they were members of the Empire, it often seemed, were the officials who ran the British Foreign Office.[44]

Another recurring theme of O Canada was, of course, Canadian politics and particularly its radical tradition, or lack thereof. In May 1929, referring to the general election then being fought in Britain, he lamented that the proposals being put forward by both Liberals and Labour would be regarded as heresy in Canada and the United States. If the ideas of J.M. Keynes and others for controlling credit and planning the economy were ever understood in North America, their effect would be as subversive as Luther's 95 Theses or Rousseau's social contract had been in their day. But there was little danger of disturbance to the Canadian status quo, if history was anything to go by. He proceeded to give his readers a version of his C H A paper and his Diamond Jubilee speeches in Saskatoon: "The prophetic fervour of

Brown in the *Globe* was succeeded by the urbane skepticism of Willison" – J.S. Willison, who had described elections as contests between the "ins" and the "outs" – "and this in turn has been replaced by the fundamentalist twaddle of the present management. The whole intellectual history of Ontario is summed up in the evolution of the *Globe*."[45] If Ontario was hopeless, the West was somewhat more promising, at least in its farmers' movements (here Underhill drew a parallel to the *Globe* of the 1860s on the Grand Trunk Railway and the Bank of Montreal), but they required an alliance with the labour movement if real progress was to be made, and this required that trade union leaders learn some lessons about political action from British labour. No political movement in history, he added in another column, had succeeded without "the driving force of class feeling behind it."[46]

The chief explanation of the weakness of radicalism in Canada, however, lay in the failure of university professors to offer farmers and workers their intellectual leadership. Instead, they worshipped at "the shrine of the god of respectability," preferring to dine with the businessmen on their universities' boards of governors than with the garage mechanics and plumbers' assistants who were (he added somewhat disingenuously) their economic equals. The eastern universities were "naturally the chief centre of this detestable form of snobbishness," but those of the west were hardly exempt from criticism. Whatever success the farmers' movements had achieved over the previous two decades had been won almost entirely without the help of the universities. The *Forum* itself offered a ray of hope in this bleak landscape, he wrote on the occasion of the journal's tenth anniversary, where "a few young men can sow their intellectual wild oats" before settling down "on the side of the angels and the bankers."[47] Underhill's rhetorical shots were nothing if not aimed equally across their entire field of fire, and his plaudits – to mix metaphors – were seldom delivered straight up, without an added slice of lemon.

This style won O Canada a wide readership in intellectual circles, combining irony, mockery, ridicule, and a professedly hard-headed realism in a way that struck a chord with the modernist mood of the 1920s. It also landed Underhill in hot water. The premier of Ontario, Howard Ferguson, complained to the chairman of the University of Toronto board of governors, Canon H.J. Cody, in April 1929, of faculty members interfering in "matters of public policy and public controversy."[48] He had already written Cody once before about allegedly anti-British statements Underhill had made in the classroom. We might be tempted simply to chalk these complaints up to "stuffy, provincial, moralistic Old Toronto" – inhospitable to the sort of Underhillism one student later recalled, that "the British flag should be made of wool so that it could shrink with the British Empire" – but they were nonetheless disquieting warnings from a political leader whose office was a stone's throw away from the university, in Queen's Park, and who also controlled the university's provincial funding.[49] Underhill was furious. He was forced to explain himself to President Falconer, who defended his faculty from political attack, but whose idea of academic freedom did not include partisan political activity or public commentary that might reflect poorly on the university. He regarded professors as analogous to judges and civil servants in their relation to public affairs.[50] This boded ill for the future, but for the moment Underhill's position was secure.

More than style was at issue, however: what Underhill had to say caused him as much trouble as the way he said it. Nothing got under the skin of those he called "those super-patriotic anti-Americans" more than his growing regard for the United States. His dispute with his new colleagues over the history program had prompted a long review essay in the *Forum*, which he had concluded by saying, "We must cease to gaze wistfully across the ocean and we must turn our energies to the vast unexplored fields which lie all around us. The greatest need of Canadian historians at present is for a Christopher

Columbus to discover America for them."[51] Canadians deceived themselves, he wrote on another occasion, in thinking they were more dignified in their comportment than Americans, when in fact they simply lacked American vitality. If they were less defensive about American influence, they might be more willing to engage in the kind of "critical realism" found in American literature and philosophy.[52] It was these kinds of sentiments that aroused the ire of Premier Ferguson. Even worse was the proposition Underhill put in an O Canada column that further involvement in European problems – which would only come as the result of Canadian investment interests, in any case – was "not worth the bones of a Toronto grenadier," a judgment that seemed to compound sacrilege on disloyalty, while casting doubt even on the prospects of the League.[53]

More generally, by the end of the twenties he had determined that his mission, in Margaret Prang's words, was "to lay bare the relationship between the economic facts of life and political power."[54] This did not mean he was an economic historian himself but that he treated politics as "only the resultant [sic] of a great complex of social, economic, and geographical forces," as he wrote in reviewing Harold Innis's *The Fur Trade in Canada*.[55] This gave all of his writing the quality of an exposé. Whatever this cost Underhill in frayed nerves, he had found his public voice.

3

Pamphleteering to Save the World

[Havelock] tells me of two other groups he has discovered in the city and who are considering the project of pamphleteering for a new social order. He thinks they might be hitched on to our movement if we catch them in time.

F.H. Underhill, 1931

The American sociologist Lewis Coser once described intellectuals as modern descendants of priests, biblical prophets, and court jesters. Surely not all at the same time, you might object. Yet, while the proportion of these different qualities might vary from one person to another, Coser's intention was to suggest that the distinctive character of intellectuals – among whom he counted himself – lay precisely in the combination of these disparate, sometimes contradictory elements.[1] They tended to the spiritual well-being of their flocks, they thundered warnings and admonitions about the state of society and its future prospects, and they took upon themselves the role of exposing pretensions and absurdities for the amusement of all who might be willing to pay attention. They might even laugh at themselves. The writer Herbert R. Lottman had much the same thing in mind in citing a description of Left Bank intellectuals in Paris during the thirties as having "certain taste for erudite clowning."[2] The last of these three qualities is the one most often forgotten by serious-minded students of "intellectuals" as a cultural type, but anyone who neglects it will miss the unique flavour of their discourse and one of the chief means by which they connected with their audience. When Underhill told Frank Scott late in 1931 that he had heard from a colleague at Toronto, the classicist Eric Havelock, that there were potential competitors in town for the "pamphleteering" role they saw for their projected "Fabian" society of political criticism, he was not only acting in character – still satiric, if no longer quite a spectator – but was communicating in a mode of irony that he knew Scott would recognize.[3]

Their "Fabian" society was what became the League for Social Reconstruction, and if J.S. Woodsworth had planted the original seed in his letter to Underhill of April 1929, it would sprout in the unlikely soil of the Berkshire Mountains in Massachusetts two years later. Underhill had begun attending the summer Institute of Politics at Williams College, in the Berkshire community of Williamstown, some years before. Initiated in 1921 by H.A. Garfield, the president of Williams, the annual gathering brought thinkers and experts on international affairs from overseas together with interested men and women from various parts of the United States and Canada. Underhill first attended in 1924, preparing ahead of time by immersing himself in the suggested background reading, and reporting afterward – having first requested approval from J.W. Dafoe – in a series of articles in the *Manitoba Free Press*. The institute routine was to hold round-table discussions in the morning, break for recreation in the afternoon – tennis, golf, swimming, "tramping" – and reassemble in the evening for a lecture by a distinguished visitor. On that first occasion, his round-table had been on the subject of problems in political theory and had been chaired by the Oxford legal historian Sir Paul Vinogradoff. Underhill found it enormously stimulating, and he returned as often as he could, in another year being thrilled to hear André Siegfried, the French sociologist and geographer, whom he described as "the most industrious and most discerning of all living students of our English-speaking democracies."[4] Siegfried was also the author of one of Underhill's favourite books, *The Race Question in Canada* (1907), which he had discovered when he was a student at Oxford.[5]

Among the attendees in 1931 was Scott, who was there for the first time. He, too, had been to Oxford, as a Rhodes Scholar in the early twenties and, like Underhill, had been dismayed by the provincial culture he found on his return. After a year teaching at Lower Canada College in Montreal, he enrolled in law at McGill University in 1924, where he joined with several kindred spirits to found the *McGill Fortnightly Review*, a journal with a sensibility not unlike that of the *Forum*, independent-minded enough to cause him and one of his fellow editors, the poet A.J.M. Smith, to be called on the carpet by the university's principal, Sir Arthur Currie. When the *Review* ran out of steam after a few years (it lasted from 1925 to 1927), Scott was one of three writers who started the even shorter-lived *Canadian Mercury* (1928–29), whose name evoked H.L. Mencken's *American Mercury*, and whose mission, announced in the first issue, was "the emancipation of Canadian literature from the state of amiable mediocrity and insipidity in which it now languishes."[6] Both journals were vehicles of the "new poetry," which in temper and form broke sharply with its Victorian predecessors. Together with Smith and a few others, Scott led the way, both as poet and critic. Poetry, he later wrote, was the route through which he entered the modern world.[7] With the onset of the Great Depression in 1929, however, his literary modernism evolved in a political direction, impelled at least in part by his deep sense of Christian duty, and perhaps nudged in that direction by memories of the English Christian socialist R.H. Tawney, whom he had met at Oxford, and whose morally charged indictment of capitalism, *The Acquisitive Society* (1920), he had read as a member of an Oxford Student Christian Union study group.[8]

When Underhill and Scott met in Williamstown, each already knew something of the other's work. Scott was a great

admirer of Underhill's O Canada columns and had contributed to the *Forum* himself, notably two pieces published earlier that year, in which he had held up the "new American
poets" as models to be followed and argued for an intellectual
affinity between modernism and socialism, both involving the
working out of new forms better adapted to the present.[9] The
two men had much in common and hit it off immediately.
One day during the meetings, Underhill suggested an afternoon picnic, and they set off, together with Percy Corbett,
dean of the McGill Faculty of Law, who had invited Scott, by
this time a professor in the faculty, to accompany him to the
institute as his secretary. Underhill lost no time in broaching
the subject of the current Depression, which he thought might
well give rise to the formation of a new party, just as had happened during the economic downturn following the war. If so,
it would need the support of a group something like the
Fabian Society if it was to have any hope of resisting the blan-
dishments of William Lyon Mackenzie King, who had wooed
many Progressives into the Liberal camp. By the time they
returned to the college, refreshed by their walk up Mount
Greylock and energized by their exchange, they had decided
to invite colleagues in both Montreal and Toronto – what
Underhill later called "unattached critical spirits" – to join
them in a new organization of intellectuals.[10] A pleasurable
afternoon's tramp had borne serious fruit.

The deteriorating state of the Canadian economy, and the damage it wrought on households across the country, left little
room for clowning, erudite or otherwise, as the Depression
deepened. In 1931, the national unemployment rate had
already reached 20 per cent; two years later, it rose to an esti-
mated 30 per cent, and while it declined thereafter, it did not
fall below 12 per cent in the remainder of the decade. The collapse of world trade meant that there was little demand for

primary products, on which the economy mainly depended, and in the case of wheat, the effect of falling prices due to glutted markets was worsened by declining production caused by drought and crop failure on the prairies. With no social safety net to speak of and governments fixated on balanced budgets – and constrained, it must be said, by the problems of divided constitutional jurisdiction – the impact on farmers and working-class families and individuals was devastating.[11] In response, various dissident groups, protest movements, and new political parties formed, and older ones found new followers.

Among the latter was the Communist Party of Canada, which had been founded after the Bolshevik Revolution as a merger of older socialist and labour parties. Neither Underhill nor Scott had any sympathy for communism – when the name of the L S R was being discussed, Scott argued for "League for Economic Democracy," partly because an emphasis on democracy would "exclude Communists" – but both found themselves defending the freedom of expression of communists when they were subjected to police action.[12] At the end of January 1931, Scott wrote a letter to the Montreal *Gazette* protesting the recent arrest, on charges of sedition, of two speakers at a meeting of the communist-run Canadian Labour Defence League. Sedition, he wrote, was ill-defined in the law, and communists, like anyone else, had a right to freedom of speech and assembly until they had committed acts in violation of the law. The *Gazette* replied that there was "no place for communism in this country," and the chief of police affirmed that he simply could not allow meetings of communists to go on in Montreal. Scott had signed himself "Associate Professor of Constitutional and Federal Law" and was criticized for doing so by Principal Currie.[13] He was at it again eighteen months later, nonetheless, in an article in *Queen's Quarterly* concerning the arrest, trial, and conviction of eight communists in Toronto in 1931, again on charges of sedition but this time explicitly on the grounds that the Communist Party was an "unlawful association" under the terms of section 98 of the Criminal Code, which had been passed in 1919 in reaction to the Winnipeg General Strike. Scott argued that section 98 itself contravened basic liberties, and that police had acted arbitrarily in raiding party offices with no apparent cause, when the party had been operating openly for seven years.[14]

In Underhill's case, his defence was less of communists themselves than of all those who were tarred as communists by authorities opposed to radicals of all kinds and threatened by the criticisms they mounted of the status quo. In January 1931, two weeks before Scott sent his letter to the *Gazette*, a branch of an international pacifist organization called the Fellowship of Reconciliation, which had established itself in Toronto eight months earlier, booked a local theatre for a discussion forum on the attitude of the Toronto Police Commission toward free speech. The topic was prompted by an earlier denial of a public hall for a meeting of the Fellowship, and by police interference with meetings more generally, some of which did involve communists. The forum was cancelled at the last minute under police pressure and was forced to meet elsewhere. Two members of the Police Commission, who had been invited to participate, called it "a communist meeting under a thin disguise." In response, Underhill and Eric Havelock drafted a letter to the four Toronto daily papers and collected signatures from sixty-six of their colleagues in the university, though none of them was identified as such. "The right of free speech and free assembly," the letter read, "is in danger of suppression in this city." It was a citizen's duty to protest, no matter how "unpopular or erroneous" the opinions expressed.[15]

The letter caused a storm of controversy. Before long, the identity of the signatories was known, and calls were heard for their discipline or dismissal. Their number included senior faculty and others whose politics were by no means uniformly liberal or radical: Donald Creighton and Chester Martin in the history department, for example; Alexander Brady and

Harold Innis in political economy; and Malcolm Wallace, Underhill's old professor from pre-war days, in English. The modern historian of both the L S R and academic freedom in Canada, Michiel Horn, has speculated that they were all probably taken aback by the violence of the reaction.[16] This may be so. Among the newspapers, only the Liberal *Toronto Daily Star* came to their defence. Underhill, as was his habit, took refuge in ridicule, collecting some of the most outrageous comments from the press and public in the *Forum* under the title – enclosed in distancing quotation marks – "'The Intellectual Capital of Canada.'" He had the most fun with the demand made by the president of the Canadian Bank of Commerce, Sir John Aird (and seconded by the Toronto *Mail and Empire*), that professors should "stick to their knitting," to which Aird had added that the failure of German professors to do the same had caused the Great War. This Underhill described as "a contribution to the vexed question of war origins which is apt to lead mere historians to wish that our banks would give their presidents some knitting to stick to."[17] In the end, the university took no action against the signatories, though public criticism by Chancellor Sir William Mulock, and a resolution passed by the board of governors dissociating the university from the letter, may have left the impression that it had done so.

It was against this background of public controversy, as well as the economic crisis, that Underhill and Scott formed their respective groups and drafted a statement of purpose for their "Fabian" society. In Toronto, the group included several who had signed the "letter of sixty-eight professors" (as it had become known), among them the economists Irene Biss and J.F. Parkinson, the historian Edgar McInnis, and the social scientist Harry M. Cassidy, as well as Underhill and Havelock. They and their colleagues in Montreal carried with them the tensions and uncertainties of the political environment, as well as the excitement of attempting to reshape it, as they put their minds to questions of organization and purpose. Their sense of embattlement may help to explain the moderation of their language. Writing in the *Forum* of the need for some nucleus of "bourgeois intellectuals" akin to those who had come to the support of the English Labour movement at the end of the nineteenth century, Underhill declared that the time was ripe for a Canadian Fabian Society to lay down a program, even if only "such a moderate programme [*sic*] as would correspond to the gas and water socialism of the original Fabians."[18] When the members of the L S R agreed on their inaugural manifesto in January 1932, at what was effectively their founding convention, held in Toronto, they made no mention of socialism at all. Instead, the manifesto declared its support for "a new social order," "a planned and socialized economy," and "an approximate economic equality among all men."[19] No doubt this omission reflected partly a desire to reach a broad range of reform-minded people, and partly a belief in the essentially liberal character of the socialism they envisioned – and perhaps too a fear among the Montrealers of alienating French Canada – but it was also true that waving the flag of socialism was only asking for trouble. Moderation was the price of legitimacy.

This was to change shortly, at least for some members, with the emergence of the C C F, but for the moment the L S R saw itself as a politically unaffiliated association, dedicated to research and education. Agreement on the specific terms of the manifesto had been reached only after much discussion within each group, as well as between them, which was not surprising for an organization seeking to define itself ideologically. After a meeting in Toronto at which a draft sent from Montreal had been discussed, Underhill reported to Scott that several of those present were "much more left-wing" than the proposed draft, but that they were more likely to accept it, in the end, than some of his "mild liberal friends" who were also present.[20] He persisted, nonetheless, with other liberal friends, sending a late draft of the manifesto to Norman MacLeod Rogers, a political scientist at Queen's who had earlier served as Mackenzie King's private secretary (and would later become a Liberal M P), inviting him to the January meeting in Toronto. Rogers declined. Though he agreed with "most" of the manifesto's objectives, he was "not ready to adopt a position of detached antagonism to the political organization to which I now give my general support."[21] As Underhill knew well enough, not all political differences could be bridged. Even after the major issues were settled, backsliding might also occur. A few months after the January meeting, he told Scott that Harry Cassidy was getting cold feet, concluding somewhat dejectedly that "at present I'm just damn tired and sick of all ideas."[22]

Still, ideas were his lifeblood. He chaired the meetings of the Toronto group and the joint meeting in January, where he was also chosen the first president of the new L S R (the Montreal group lost the argument over the association's name). Between himself and Scott, he was undoubtedly the primary leader, perhaps partly because of his seniority in age – he was ten years older than most of the others – as well as the fertility of his mind, and while the manifesto itself was not his alone, its diagnosis of the problems of the time was one he shared wholeheartedly. "The present capitalist system," the preamble declared, "has shown itself unjust and inhuman, economically wasteful, and a standing threat to peace and democratic government." The concentration of power in the hands of a small minority, and the degradation of the vast majority, were inherent in a system based on private profit. There followed a list of ten measures that were necessary "first steps" toward a new order. These included creation of a National Planning Commission, socialization of "the machinery of banking and investment," public ownership of industries "approaching a condition of monopoly," development of co-operative institutions where appropriate, and the establishment of boards to regulate foreign trade. It also called for social legislation to protect workers (e.g., insurance against unemployment, illness, and old age), publicly organized health services, an "aggressive" taxation policy to raise revenues and reduce income inequality, amendment of the constitution to give the Dominion government powers to deal with national economic problems, and a foreign policy "designed to obtain international economic co-operation and to promote disarmament and world peace."[23] This was a radical agenda, no less so for laying out a program, parts of which would become conventional wisdom over the next half-century without leading to the new social order that the L S R envisioned.

Later that year, Underhill revealed the basis of his thinking as fully as he ever did at the time in a brilliant revisionist essay on the English philosopher and political theorist Jeremy Bentham, published in *Queen's Quarterly*. The essay – a form better suited to his mode of thought than the manifesto – conveyed his sense of historical change and continuity, as well as his understanding of what "Bentham and Benthamism" meant for the present. He began by making a connection between the "bourgeois revolution" of the early nineteenth century, of which Bentham had been the philosopher, and the coming end of bourgeois rule, "as a new era painfully emerges out of the confusion and suffering of our own revolutionary period." Notoriously the proponent of utilitarianism, in which the good of any public action was to be measured by the "greatest happiness of the greatest number," and an adherent of Adam Smith's principle that the sum total of individual interests, freely pursued, would amount to the common good, Bentham also became a believer in political democracy as the only system of government in which the "greatest happiness" principle could be achieved. This led him to propose various reforms of public administration and public education, without which the mass of the people could not become the rational calculators that democracy required. He and his followers pursued a series of reforms, including the Factory Act of 1833, which regulated the hours of work of children and provided for factory inspectors. It was "the first nail in the coffin of *laissez-faire*" and an act,

Underhill wrote, that "began the process that was to lead to the collectivist state."

Never in this process, however, even as it was picked up and carried forward by the Fabians later in the century, was the core belief in individual liberty – in the "free development of personality" – abandoned. Underhill quoted a prominent Fabian of the late nineteenth and early twentieth centuries, who was also himself a British colonial administrator, to the effect that "Socialism is merely Individualism rationalized, organized, clothed, and in its right mind." (He might also have recalled Hobhouse's rather more sedate formulation of the same notion: "The ideas of socialism, when translated into practical terms, coincide with the ideas to which Liberals are led when they seek to apply their principles of Liberty, Equality, and the Common Good to the industrial life of our time."[24]) Then, moving his argument onto another plane entirely, Underhill concluded that Benthamism was therefore not opposed to collectivism, but it *was* opposed to the "worship of the state" to which certain forms of socialism were prone: "Perhaps the permanent contribution of Bentham," he wrote, "is the hard realistic temper, coldly analytical, completely unmystical, which he applied to the solution of political problems." Adoption of such an outlook would inoculate one against the mystical notion that one ought to subordinate one's will to that of the state, for the sake of one's own good, as in Italian Fascism, or to the dictatorship of the proletariat, as in Russian Communism. This was not an argument in support of Benthamite atomistic individualism, but for a new Benthamism adapted to contemporary needs that would bring a "wider social vision" to the maximizing of individual happiness.[25] Here was Underhill's conception of socialism, and much of it was embodied in the L S R manifesto.

Whatever uncertainties he had about how the League's ideas might find their way into the political arena were removed when news arrived in the summer of 1932 that a meeting of farm and labour groups in Calgary had created a new party, the Co-operative Commonwealth Federation, fulfilling his earlier hope for such an eventuality that he had expressed to Scott at Williams College. The formation of the CCF represented the culmination of meetings, conversations, and informal alliances among western farm and labour parties and organizations that had been going on for some time. Those groups included the United Farmers of Alberta, then the governing party in Alberta, which had called the meeting in Calgary, and the parliamentary Ginger Group, among whose members Woodsworth was especially important. Universally respected by all of the participants, he became the "linchpin" holding them all together and making possible a more or less united front.[26] This was no small feat, as the CCF's federal structure and full name – CCF (Farmer-Labour-Socialist) – reflected the refusal of the various participants to bury their differences entirely in a complete merger. The coalition structure would cause problems down the road and was something Underhill could never fully understand. When the party later fell short of expectations, he urged Woodsworth to centralize party operations and impose his will more forcibly on his recalcitrant followers, but Woodsworth insisted on local control, one instance in which the "saintly" leader demonstrated a surer grasp of political realities than his intellectual advisor, to whom he otherwise frequently turned for advice on policy.[27]

Perhaps the most important occasion on which he sought Underhill's aid was at the very beginning, when he asked him and other members of the LSR to draft a party manifesto. The request revealed an LSR that was not without its own divisions and contradictions. When Underhill heard of the party's formation, his immediate reaction was to think that the LSR ought to affiliate, in the same way as the farm and labour parties had.[28] Wasn't this just what he and his colleagues had wanted? Wasn't Woodsworth already honorary president of the LSR (on Underhill's invitation)? But as discussion ensued over the following months, it became apparent that this was a minority view. Scott, for one, was opposed, firmly informing one correspondent that the League was "a purely educational organization."[29] Others thought the L S R had established itself on a moderate, ecumenical basis and did not want to see it move further left. Even Woodsworth was hesitant, fearing that members who were civil servants, for example, or who had joined thinking the L S R's purpose was educational, would leave if it became more expressly partisan.[30] Yet, this did not stop him from requesting help in formulating a party platform, and L S R leaders, for their part, jumped at the chance, despite their hesitations about official affiliation. It was the sort of work, Scott rationalized, that they could do "without involving the League as a whole."[31]

The job was taken on by the L S R Research Committee, which had been struck to organize the writing of a book – eventually completed and published as *Social Planning for Canada* (1935) – that would diagnose the ills of Canadian capitalism and prescribe remedies. Underhill undertook the task of writing the first draft, which he did not produce until mid-June 1933, rather late in the day considering the C C F convention was scheduled to open a month later, but he always worked best under pressure. Using the L S R manifesto as his model, he came up with a version very much like it, which he then revised in cooperation with three other members of the committee and sent off to colleagues who would take it to Regina: Woodsworth, Joseph Parkinson, a member of the committee who was going as an observer, and Scott, who was also attending the convention. Two other Montreal members attended as delegates of the city's C C F Council, Eugene Forsey and J. King Gordon, both of them founding members of the L S R, and both of them politically active members of the Montreal academic community. In Regina, the Toronto draft was discussed prior to the convention at meetings of the C C F National Council, at which the four L S R members were present, and at the convention itself. While numerous changes were made, the final manifesto did not depart significantly in its philosophy or specific proposals from that of the LSR, though it expanded considerably on their rationale. Although the more Marxist-oriented labour parties from British Columbia and the more moderate farmers' representatives, notably from Ontario, objected – the one to the document's liberal reformism, the other to its radical socialism – it passed with only one dissenting vote. The LSR had "scored a brilliant success," Scott reported.[32] Meanwhile, George Ferguson, a journalist with the *Winnipeg Free Press*, dubbed the LSR the CCF's "brain trust."[33] So much for formal nonaffiliation.

———

Reviewing Herbert Butterfield's *The Whig Interpretation of History* (1931) in the *Forum* in June 1932, Underhill praised the book for its "brilliant onslaught" on the tendency of historians to judge the past against the values of the present. He agreed with Butterfield that it was "the whole of the past," in all its complexity, that produced "the whole of the present," and that the past ought not to be seen as a linear progression to one's own time. Yet, he also wondered if Butterfield was not more concerned with the sins of actual Whigs in this regard, to the neglect of Tories who did the same thing, and he pointed out that Butterfield's "glorification of disinterested scientific research" was addressed to "English readers in a country whose historians have always been half politicians." Coincidentally, the American historian Carl Becker had given his presidential address to the American Historical Association at about the same time as Butterfield's book had come out, and Becker had just as brilliantly criticized the dominance in his own country of the German ideal of pure research that Butterfield seemed to be recommending. There was no doubt where Underhill stood: "The truth is that all the great historians from Thucydides to the present have been men who lived intensely in their own age and who brought their own intense sense of values to the interpretation of the material on which they worked." The dull PhDs differed from them only in their own dullness. Historians, he concluded, must strive to be conscious and critical of their own values, but they could not escape them.[34]

This outlook – his philosophy of history – and the intensity of his own commitments were evident in a succession of longer articles and essays that Underhill wrote through the 1930s. He found local precedent for his posture of engagement in the Victorian liberal, Goldwin Smith, who had been a presence in his life for many years, at least since he had served as an usher at the old man's sparsely attended funeral in Convocation Hall at the university in 1910. His interest had deepened as he found in Smith many of the same qualities of independent-mindedness and contrariness that he admired in John Stuart Mill and George Bernard Shaw, which were all the more resonant since Smith was nominally a historian. In an essay written in 1933, the same year as his Bentham piece, Underhill traced Smith's life and thought from his years in England, where he had criticized the clerical control of Oxford University, and where he had embarked on his career as a controversialist – becoming a "pamphleteer" – to his move, first to Cornell University in upstate New York, and then to Toronto, where he had spent the last thirty-nine years of his life discovering that "the influence which an intellectual can exercise in Canadian public affairs is severely limited." Underhill did not share Smith's belief, expressed most famously in *Canada and the Canadian Question* (1891), that Canada's destiny lay in union with the United States, but he did agree that his country was "an American democracy." He also admired Smith's association with the Canada First movement and thought that the political criticism that flowed from his pen under the byline of "A Bystander" was a model of "high-class independent journalism," unique in its time. Everything Smith wrote had been informed by his knowledge of international intellectual movements and ideas. It had been his sad fate to reside "in a city which, while it respected him highly for his attainments, abhorred his political views and never made much attempt to understand him."[35] Biography here joined with autobiography.

Underhill's philosophy was evident, as well, as he developed and applied ideas about Canadian party history that he had first put forward in Saskatoon in the mid-twenties, the shifting tones and emphases of which were inseparable from the politics of contemporary Canada, the United States, and Europe. In 1932, after the LSR had formed but before the CCF, he delivered a paper to the annual meeting of the Canadian Political Science Association (CPSA) that did not so much advance his ideas as apply them with greater urgency. His central proposition was that Canadian parties became more American in character after Confederation, despite their British-derived names, functioning as instruments of conciliation among the diverse "racial and sectional" groups loosely held together in the new and expanding Dominion, rather than as proponents of ideas that might have offered real choice to the electorate. John A. Macdonald had led the way in this process, defining the height of statesmanship as the bringing together of representatives of the militantly Protestant Orange Order and the ultramontane Quebec Catholic Church to the same cabinet table. Laurier, before whom the Liberal party had been "cursed with principle and ... unable to attain office except accidentally," transformed the party into a clone of the Conservatives, thereby giving it a new "sophistication," not to mention success at the polls. The result was to "enthrone insincerity in our national politics" and make it possible for powerful interest groups – the Catholic Church and big business – to exercise control behind the scenes, while the parties themselves became vote-getting machines.[36]

The class control of Canadian politics, Underhill argued, had evoked counter-class responses in the form of the farmers' and labour movements of the 1920s. While they had not succeeded, they had shown that it was possible for politics to be about something other than attaining immediate office. And here was the lesson for the moment. The Depression had demonstrated the failure of profit-seeking business concerns, pursuing their own interests, to achieve stable economic development and had shown the need for political control: "If democracy cannot organize its economic life, the necessary task of organization will be taken over by other forms of government. Russia and Italy provide us with alternative methods, and neither of them admits of the parliamentary institutions to which we are accustomed."[37] It was a warning that he would reiterate later that year in his Bentham essay. What was now at stake was not merely party success, or even the fate of any particular party measure, but democracy itself.

Three years later, in 1935, he put historical flesh on the bones of his main idea, appropriately enough in the pages of the *Canadian Historical Review*. Grounding his analysis in James Madison's tenth Federalist paper, written in 1787 in support of the proposed new US constitution, Underhill argued that political parties were best understood as expressions of material interest. He did so almost certainly guided by his reading of Charles Beard's *Economic Interpretation of the Constitution of the United States* a decade earlier.[38] "The most common and durable source of factions," Madison had written, "has been the various and unequal distribution of property." Underhill set this up against the rather vapid proposition of Mackenzie King's that politics was a struggle between "the principle of the future and the principle of the past," which Underhill called the idealist approach, in contrast to Madison's realism.

He proceeded to trace the origins of the Canadian system to the coalition of Tories and certain so-called moderate Reformers that Macdonald had formed in 1854, creating the Liberal-Conservative party and relegating other Reformers – Grits, Brownites, and Lower Canadian *Rouges* – to the margin. Describing the components of both parties in pre-Confederation Canada and how they later established themselves as the parties of the Dominion, he explained the workings of Macdonald's Hamiltonian politics – named after Alexander Hamilton, the business-friendly, centralizing, closet monarchist of the early American republic – and contrasted them with the Jeffersonian politics of the pre-Laurier Liberals – Thomas Jefferson being the personification of American agrarian democracy and Hamilton's opposite number in political combat. He summed up the system that emerged – business purposes concealed by sectional bargaining – in imagery quoted from Goldwin Smith: "Sir John Macdonald may be the Prince of Darkness; with some of its imps he is certainly far too familiar. But an angel of light would perhaps have not been so successful in holding together the motley and discordant elements, local, ethnological, religious, social and personal" that together constituted the Dominion.[39] The system reached its apogee in the reciprocity election of 1911, which showed the power of Toronto business to get its way when it felt threatened, but which also gave rise to the reincarnation of old Upper Canadian agrarian radicalism in "the new West."

In two other pieces published that year, he redirected his argument, on the one hand putting it expressly in the service of electing a socialist party, in his contribution on "The Question of Parties" to *Social Planning for Canada*, on the other using it as a basis for asking who and what defined Canada's "national interest." In the LSR volume, he gave readers a short course on the nature of parties in general and their history in Canada in particular. The CCF, he argued, offered Canadians the only real hope of dealing with the current crisis of monopoly capitalism. Not only was it class-based – farmers and labour, plus professional men and women whose knowledge and skills were essential to the making of a socialist state – but it was also dedicated to the propagation of ideas and the education of the electorate, which were the real historic functions of a political party. Though he did not say so, this had also been the conception of party held by the Radical Clear Grits of the previous century, necessarily updated to take account of modern organizational needs. In a long aside, amounting to some eight pages of the article's total twenty-five-page length, he subjected the program of the recently formed League for National Government to detailed criticism. Purporting to be above politics, it was actually a vehicle of business interests, at best, and potentially fascist, at worst.[40]

Underhill's discussion of the national interest, in another paper delivered to the annual meeting of the C P S A (and originating in another idea drawn from his reading of Beard, this time *The Idea of National Interest*, published in 1934), began with the idealism of the Canada First movement of the 1870s, whose attempt to transcend particular interests foundered on its own Ontario-centredness. For all of its idealist aspirations, it had been "a sectional movement clothing itself in the impressive garments of nationalism." Similarly, in the present day, numerous spokesmen for regional interests, including many political scientists, were proposing to locate the cause of the failure of governments to respond effectively to the Depression in the federal structure of Canada. While, to some extent, this was not an unreasonable response to the long domination of Dominion politics by Hamiltonian parties, Underhill thought the obsession with political forms, rather than their underlying economic foundations, was a mark of "the modern bourgeois liberal mind." The problem was capitalism, not federalism. Propositions to the contrary were only the latest of many deceptive rationalizations that had achieved the status of conventional wisdom in a process Walter Lippmann had explained, "with great insight and subtlety," in his book *Public Opinion* (1922), and from whose grip the country was in need of emancipation. Expressions of the national interest could not be separated from their class origins.[41]

Canadian academics, he continued, were prominent among those who would have people think otherwise. Economists, for example, never questioned the structure and purpose of capitalism; instead, they tinkered with its machinery, "doing occasional repair jobs on Royal commissions, such as putting new brake linings into the financial mechanism, happy in their unambitious way [to serve] as the intellectual garage-mechanics of Canadian capitalism." For their part, historians avoided the grease and grime of the workshop, preferring the front office, "helping to sell the system to the public with a slick line of talk about responsible government and national autonomy."[42] In the space of a few pages, Underhill took swipes at his colleagues in political science, economics, and history. Harold Innis, no stranger to royal commissions, surely had this in the back of his mind when he reviewed *Social Planning for Canada* in the *University of Toronto Quarterly* the following year. He suggested that, in a new country where the rewards of serious scholarship were few and economic fluctuations caused by dependence on raw materials were great, and where ignorance of economics was widespread, "footloose adventurers turn in some cases to business and its profits during booms, and in others to political activity and popular acclaim during depressions" for compensation. "Volubility" was often confused with "intellectual interest."[43] While identifying no one by name, there was little doubt of at least one of the persons to whom he was referring.

Underhill, in turn, lost no time in responding in the *Canadian Forum*. He began by noting that university professors had long played a central role in European politics, which (by the way) helped to explain the vitality of European writing on history, economics, and law, compared to similar writing in North America: "But to the business men of this country universities are still very much like Dutch paintings; they are things to which you point with pride as the proof of culture, especially of its expensiveness; but they have no part in the world of practical affairs." In fact, in Great Britain, which was otherwise held up as worthy of Canada's emulation, and even in Canada itself, the "academic man" was no stranger to politics. Why, then, was his involvement now protested? Could it be because of his newly pink coloration? No sooner had he put this decidedly rhetorical question than he turned his guns from the business enemy onto his fellow academics, whose pretense to Olympian detachment he attacked just as vigorously. There were risks, he allowed, in partisanship, "but in trying to avoid them it is not necessary to go to the other extreme and become a fussy academic old maid always in terror lest the virginal purity of one's scientific mind be exposed to indecent assault if one ventures into the rude world."[44] The other tendencies, he added, to which academics were prone were simple indecision – a failure to climb off the fence on one side or the other – and the lure of respectability, which too many, especially economists, pursued before all else. He was fully in his take-no-prisoners mode.

———————

Underhill's provocative, sometimes abrasive style was one he cultivated with the encouragement of friends and readers. Years earlier, in the autumn of 1929, Graham Spry, who was then national secretary of the Association of Canadian Clubs, had invited him to speak at a club meeting, adding, "the more critical, the better"; and early in 1931, shortly after he had visited Montreal to give a talk, Brooke Claxton, who had been his host for much of the time, reported that people were trying to quote "some of your more pungent phrases, failing dismally." Claxton was an active member of the Canadian Club of Montreal and the local League of Nations Society, and was one of a group of young cultural nationalists that had formed around Frank Scott and his wife, Marion. A few months later, Kingsley Martin, editor of the *New Statesman and Nation* in England, thanked Underhill for a piece he had sent them on Canada and the Great Depression and told him more like it would be welcome: "May I say that the more bold and outspoken you are the better pleased I shall be?" It was good to upset people a little.[45]

Style was one axis along which Underhill connected with his readers, and in the 1920s and 1930s, as we have noted, sarcasm, mockery, skepticism, and derision were the common currency of intellectual criticism. One would not use such terms to describe the language and temper of the sage in an earlier era. W.D. LeSueur, for example, also wrote about social and intellectual questions in the 1870s and 1880s, but he did so in long, dense, complex sentences and paragraphs, in which he deployed the imagery of truth, beauty, and nobility of soul. Underhill's prose was cooler and cleaner – "crisp, idiomatic, and epigrammatic," in the words of the literary historian Desmond Pacey – and his categories were historical and relativist, rather than universal or absolute.[46]

There were other axes of connection as well, including the gendered language evident in his invoking of the "fussy academic old maid" as a type especially to be scorned. Underhill's view of women, in fact, verged on the misogynist, for all the encouragement he gave to students such as Hilda Neatby and Margaret Prang. Reporting on the Williamstown summer institute to the *Manitoba Free Press* in 1929, he had informed his readers that one of the few drawbacks of an otherwise stimulating environment had been the presence of too many women of the man-hunting and bridge-playing type, who only served to confirm one's prejudice "that the female of the species is incapable of politics."[47] It wasn't entirely clear that they were capable of studying history, either. Apart from the comments he had made when he first discovered young women in his classes at the University of Saskatchewan, he complained at Toronto of the tendency of arts courses to become "female preserves" as a result of the growing popularity of commerce courses among male students. Aside from a few professors ("peacocks") who enjoyed performing for females, he had told a conference on university education in 1930, "no University teacher wants to be condemned to teach women."[48] Despite the presence of a few women in the LSR, like Irene Biss, or on the board of the *Forum*, like Eleanor Godfrey and (for a time) Dorothy Livesay, intellectual discourse about politics, for Underhill and most of his friends and readers, was an extension of masculine conversation into the public realm.

At the same time, many found his style irritating, among them sometimes the same people who were otherwise stimulated by it. One *Forum* reader wrote in to complain of excessive gloominess and "destructive criticism" in the journal's columns, singling out "F.H.U." as one of the guilty parties. "F.H.U." was unrepentant, devoting an entire O Canada column to explaining the necessity of criticism in journals like the *Forum*, whose purpose was "exploding popular delusions and exposing the quacks who preach them."[49] Closer to home, Frank Scott wrote Harry Cassidy early in 1935, asking him for his revised chapter in the forthcoming LSR book – Cassidy had moved to Victoria to become the provincial director of social welfare in British Columbia – and reporting on the recent convention: rather gloomy, he said, with "Underhill in his best pessimistic mood," to which Cassidy replied that, whatever their friend's "many excellencies," he was not "a person who inspires enthusiasm in those of uncertain faith."[50]

More sharply, and more directly, Scott wrote a long letter to Underhill early in the following year, strongly objecting to a piece he had written in the *Forum* criticizing a convocation address delivered at the University of Western Ontario by Sir Edward Beatty, the president of the Canadian Pacific Railway and chancellor of McGill. Responding to the publication of *Social Planning for Canada*, Beatty had gone after professors of economics for taking up the cause of socialism. Underhill had reacted by accusing Beatty of red-baiting. Or was his real concern that some economists – otherwise tame creatures of the system as it stood – were critical of his plans to take over Canadian National Railways? And what about his sinister suggestion that universities might not survive popular discontent? If this was not "an invitation for some Canadian would-be Hitler to work up a demagogic agitation against our schools and universities," what was it? It was foolhardy, Scott said, to start a fight with the C P R. Friends at McGill, potential supporters of the L S R, were now distancing themselves from it.[51]

Revealing broader underlying concerns, Scott went on to suggest that it was time for the *Forum* to move beyond the negative criticism and "stock grievances" of the early thirties to a more positive stance, praising small steps forward, encouraging its friends – even Liberal sympathizers – and proposing constructive plans for the future. We ought to become "enthusiasts," he wrote, "uplifters, and Babbitts in a socialist way." Underhill was having none of it, though he did apologize for maligning Eustace Morgan, the principal of McGill, in his column, on the basis of a rumour that had come from someone he had thought was a reliable source. The poor showing of the C C F in the 1935 election, he contended, which Mackenzie King's Liberals had won decisively, made it all the more important to analyze Liberal policies with a critical eye. There was an obvious remedy, of course, for those who thought that the *Forum* needed to accentuate the positive: they could write for it themselves. "But I am not going to become any damned combination of Christian apostle and American Babbitt," he concluded, "for the sake of converting a few distressed members of the Montreal bourgeoisie."

The exchange was more heated than any the two men had at the time, yet there was nothing about it that threatened their personal relations. Underhill's reply also dealt with some L S R business and solicited a contribution to the *Forum* from Scott, ending by inviting him to stay with the Underhills for the upcoming L S R convention. The intensity of political debate among everyone involved in the *Forum*, the L S R, and the C C F did not permanently disrupt friendships, for the most part. This is all the more striking in light of the *Forum*'s instability in the thirties. J.M. Dent and Sons withdrew as publisher in April 1934, partly because the journal was a drain on scarce funds, and perhaps also because of the more

distinctly socialist posture it had adopted in the past two
years.[52] The succeeding ownership by Steven Cartwright, a
young Liberal, prompted a withdrawal of former editors and
contributors, including Underhill, but it didn't last. Cartwright
sold the *Forum* to Graham Spry a year later, for one dollar
(debts were included in the purchase price), and the old hands
returned, planning to make the journal, in Underhill's words,
"more definitely socialist."[53] For all of Spry's journalistic
experience, however, there was little resulting improvement,
at least on the business side. In April 1936, Underhill reported
to Scott that he was "fed up with Graham," and a month later
Eleanor Godfrey, who at this point was looking after the
Forum's office, complained of "Graham's irresponsible behaviour," adding that Underhill was threatening to resign and
she was afraid that he might actually do so. George Grube,
a Trinity College classicist who was active in the L S R and
C C F, and a member of the editorial board, agreed with
Godfrey's assessment.[54]

Things settled down a little, at least for a time, when Spry
relinquished control to the L S R shortly afterward, on the
same terms as he had acquired it. The League took over the
journal after careful consideration, partly on the basis of its
own improved financial status as a result of royalties for *Social
Planning for Canada*, and partly because Carlton McNaught,
a Toronto advertising executive and quiet supporter of the
L S R and C C F, provided financial backing to the tune of
$1,000. One condition of his support was that Underhill, an
old friend since their undergraduate days at the University of
Toronto, return to an active editorial role.[55] Nevertheless, the
journal remained very much a hand-to-mouth operation, subject to recurring financial crises. Early in the following year,
Mark Farrell, a young commerce graduate who had been
hired as business manager, wrote a long report for the L S R
executive on the state of the journal. Although its financial
situation had not really improved, the more serious problems
were editorial, he thought, especially the strained relations

among members of the board. One person needed to be put in charge. Of all the candidates, Underhill was the best writer, "but is in a state of sulkiness for which he has my complete sympathy." Others included Grube (the hardest worker but somewhat "heavy" in his tastes), Havelock (unreliable), Spry (excellent contacts but influence negligible), and Earle Birney (the "best person after Underhill"). Birney, who was teaching medieval English literature at Toronto and making a name for himself as a poet, had joined the board a few months before. Farrell's recommendation was that Underhill be appointed "editor in chief with full powers."[56]

The executive agreed, and Scott wrote Underhill in late February 1937 to ask if he would take on the job, reserving the right to criticize "when you have twisted your knife too viciously in some unfortunate victim." After hesitating at first, Underhill acquiesced.[57] Since McNaught had come to the journal's rescue, he had been writing six, seven, eight, and more pieces per issue – editorial items, articles, and reviews – and he continued to do so. Looking back on his editorship many years later, Humphrey Carver, a community planner who had joined the editorial board on the invitation of Spry, affectionately recalled monthly Sunday evening sessions of the board at the Underhills', putting the final touches on the next issue, Ruth Underhill keeping everyone going with refreshments, "while Frank's devastating and witty commentary on the current political scene provided the background."[58] Earle Birney had similarly fond memories. His Trotskyist political views were distinctly out of step with those of his colleagues, but he recalled that Underhill had been "shrewd enough and informed enough" to know that this meant he "did not accept the Stalinist notion that a piece of writing was better *because* it was written by a proletarian or even by virtue of its being about one," which was the aesthetic of the Marxist journal, *New Masses*. At the same time, Birney understood that he was to stick to his cobbler's last – the literary matters that became his responsibility when he was appointed literary editor. Despite the differences that did occur, "bonds of friendship and mutual esteem" drew everyone together in the joint enterprise of producing something "at least vaguely like a Canadian *New Statesman*."[59]

Those bonds were all the closer for the frequent socializing among the overlapping groups of people connected with the *Forum*, the CCF, and the LSR. One of the social centres was McNaught's house on Blythwood Road in Lawrence Park, a genteel setting, one might think, for gatherings of dangerous socialists. In the memory of McNaught's son Kenneth, his home's living room served as an intellectual salon, the "towering" Scott, visiting from Montreal, engaging in lively discussion with the "diminutive" Underhill, joined by "the sparky redhead" Godfrey, "the owl-like" Northrop Frye, a "glowering" Grube, and others – Eugene Forsey, Escott Reid, Douglas LePan, David Lewis, Saul Rae, and Harry Cassidy – whose fellowship underlay their intellectual and political activism.[60] Nevertheless, Underhill resigned only eight months after he took on the job, exhausted, he thought, of ideas, and also, one imagines, of energy. Early in 1938, he drastically cut back on his contributions for a period of about nine months.[61] By the end of the year, he was back at it, unable to stay away.

4

Reorientation

I think with deference that by a proper exercise of verbal
definition it seems more likely that you are a liberal than
I am a socialist.

Stuart Garson to Frank Underhill, 1947

Underhill's most serious problems of conflict in the 1930s
were not with friends or colleagues, but with authority, academic and political, and the press. Hardly a year went by that
he was not called to account by the university president,
prompted, as often as not, by a call from Queen's Park or an
irate member of the board of governors, or by an outraged
editorial in the Toronto *Globe*, the *Mail and Empire*, or the
Telegram. In 1932, Sir Robert Falconer was succeeded as president by Canon H.J. Cody, who had served the previous nine
years as chairman of the board of governors. As Underhill's
thinking on the subjects of the Empire and the League of
Nations grew more radical – one's place on the political spectrum in the 1930s was defined as much by one's stance on
foreign policy as by one's view of politics or the relations of
production – tensions escalated between him and Cody. In
1933, he was required to sever his relations with the CCF
clubs, which were associations designed to recruit men and
women to the party cause who were not otherwise members
of unions or farmers' organizations, and in the establishment
of which he at first played an active part. In the fall of that
year, he gave a speech in Orillia, under the auspices of the

university's extension department, in which he expressed his growing concern that Canada would be caught up in another European war – Adolf Hitler having taken control of Germany in March – because of its relationship to Britain. Reports of his speech moved from the local Orillia paper to the *Mail and Empire* to Cody's office, and Underhill had to promise to be more temperate. It was the last extension lecture he gave.[1] On this occasion, he also heard from his old mentor, G.M. Wrong, who admonished him to abandon "partisan propaganda" in favour of serious historical research. "The partisan spirit," wrote Wrong, "is disloyal to truth."[2]

The following year, he spoke at the second annual Couchiching Conference, the summer meeting of the Canadian Institute on Economics and Politics, declaring both the Empire and the League to be irrelevant to Canada and rueing Canada's participation in the Great War. Temperate it was not. In November he gave a talk in London, Ontario, in which he declared: "We went into war blindly because we swallowed the British propaganda about democracy."[3] This time, Cody extracted a promise from him that he would make no public speeches for a year. He was also placed under R C M P surveillance.[4] There followed a period in which he confined himself to print, sometimes anonymously in the *Forum*, but in 1937 he aroused the anger of the newly merged *Globe and Mail* when he complained during a C B C radio debate that, over breakfast, he was now forced to read whatever two gold-mining millionaires – a reference to the owner of the new paper, William Wright, and its publisher, George McCullagh – saw fit to provide him. The newspaper demanded his dismissal, and he was called in once again by Cody. This proved, in the end, to be another dodged bullet.

Now, however, an earlier piece of writing returned to haunt him. In *Social Planning for Canada*, he had written the final version of the chapter on foreign policy (as well as the one on political parties). In it, he had painted a bleak picture of the prospects for peace, certainly if they depended on the actions of Britain and the other European powers. It was becoming clear, he had written, that the postwar period was over, and a new pre-war period had begun. The challenge for Canada was to avoid finding itself dragged willy-nilly into another war because it had failed to define its commitments to the two international organizations of which it was a member, the Empire and the League. Reviewing the country's foreign policy under Laurier and Sir Robert Borden, and in the years since, he wrote that war was simply a permanent condition of capitalist civilization, and that Canada would be unable to resist the siren call of "democracy" or "international law" or "collective sanctions" until it had embarked on its own reconstruction. Far from the League – much less the Empire – proving its usefulness in regulating international relations in any way that conflicted with the interests of its leading members, those members had returned to pre-1914 balance-of-power diplomacy. In the circumstances, neutrality was the only sensible course for Canada: "We should therefore make clear to London and to Geneva that we intend to fertilize no more crops of poppies blooming in Flanders fields."[5] A similar policy of avoiding entanglements also had to be followed with respect to the United States in its relations with China and Japan.

Underhill had written much the same thing, though concluding with even more inflammatory language, in a memorandum on foreign policy prepared for a meeting of the Canadian Institute of International Affairs (CIIA) in 1935, and the conclusion had found its way into a book by R.A. MacKay and E.B. Rogers, *Canada Looks Abroad*, published in 1938, in a section describing isolationism as a policy alternative.[6] The passage quoted in the book became a subject of public controversy when George Drew, leader of the Conservative opposition in the Ontario legislature, raised it in April 1939 during a debate concerning similar statements made by George Grube. Underhill quickly became the focus of attention, this being only the latest in a series of indiscreet

public declarations he had made. The sentence about fertilizing no more poppies prompted a cry of "Shame! Shame!"
from Premier Mitchell Hepburn across the aisle. Neither man
seemed to be aware that it had also appeared in *Social
Planning for Canada*, nor that the last sentence of the offending paragraph – "All these European troubles are not worth
the bones of a Toronto grenadier" – was also recycled, in this
case from an O Canada column of 1929 that we noted earlier.[7] This was just as well, since their ignorance made it possible for Underhill later to defend himself, in part, on the
grounds that the passage originated in an internal document
of the CIIA and had been quoted without his knowledge.
What mattered to Drew, and to others, was the disloyalty they
thought the words expressed, and the danger their author –
and Grube – posed to susceptible young minds. Hepburn
wondered aloud why the university board of governors had
not disciplined Underhill before this; if it did not, he would
have to consider acting himself.[8]

It was no coincidence that Dr Herbert Bruce, a member of
the board and a prominent Conservative, as well as former
Ontario lieutenant-governor, brought the quotation to a special meeting of the board held on the very same day as the
debate in the legislature. Cody was instructed to find out
what Underhill had to say for himself. In the rather tense
interview that followed, Underhill questioned the fairness of
bringing up a statement he had made four years before – in a
private document – as if it were a judgment of contemporary
affairs. Moreover, the statement had come at the end of a
lengthy analysis of Canadian foreign relations since 1914
and was no reflection on Canada's soldiers in the war, of
whom he had been one: "The sentence meant simply, as its
whole context showed, that events since 1918 had convinced
me that the fact that we had buried 60,000 Canadians in
Europe in that war was a very good reason why we should
not bury more of them in Europe in another war." He
acknowledged that his wording had been offensive to many

and regretted "having expressed myself in this way." He also protested that he had been careful in his public statements, as he had undertaken to be, in the two years since he had last met with the president. He could not guarantee that anything he would say in the future would be immune to being taken out of context for the purpose of attacking him, but he would do his best to behave "as reasonable men would expect a professor to behave."[9]

Cody explained all this in a long memorandum to the board, adding an outline of Underhill's war record (which Underhill had provided him) and an account of the nature of academic freedom based in part on statements of Robert Hutchins, president of the University of Chicago. Their own university, he wrote, "enjoyed a full measure of academic freedom," accompanied by a "responsibility to use that freedom with wisdom and good taste." He expressed confidence in his professorial staff and student body, who ought not to be judged by the views of "a very few unwise and fanatical professors." This was hardly a ringing endorsement of the right to dissent, but he had secured Underhill's agreement that the purpose of a university was to search for truth, and that all expression ought to be marked by "dignity, good taste and the decent restraints of scholarship." In conclusion, he recommended that the board take no further action.[10] In arriving at his recommendation, Cody had been influenced by a student petition in defence of free speech, and by statements in support of Underhill from faculty, including Chester Martin (who nevertheless had thought the quoted passage "indefensible and unworthy of a scholar in Mr. Underhill's position"), W.P.M. Kennedy, one of Underhill's former history colleagues and now head of the law school, and Harold Innis. Underhill was saved again, though his fate had been by no means certain. "I was pretty well scared this time," he wrote Scott in May, "and lost sleep over it." He had agreed to keep quiet, but the result was that "these damned reactionaries" would win in the end. A few months later he added that, according to gossip "downtown," he was being watched by the police and was to be interned.[11]

The final chapter was still to come. On 23 August 1940, he participated in a panel discussion, again at Couchiching, on "A United American Front," an especially timely subject in view of the announcement a few days earlier of an agreement between Prime Minister Mackenzie King and US president Franklin Roosevelt to create a Permanent Joint Board of Defence between the two countries. The Ogdensburg Agreement, as it came to be known, provided a mechanism for advising the two governments on matters related to their common defence, which had become especially urgent with the advance of the Axis powers in Europe, and particularly the evacuation of Allied forces from Dunkirk and the fall of France in May and June. Underhill did not read from a prepared text, but he did write one retrospectively, in response to a request from President Cody two weeks later. It reads today as a calm and judicious assessment of the new state of affairs – there were no references to fertilizing poppies, or any similar incendiary phrases – and so it was regarded by most of his listeners. It was ironic, he said (recognizing the difficulties of appreciating irony under the circumstances), that only a year before, Canada's entry into the war had seemed to underscore the identity of its interests with those of Great Britain, yet the recent agreement suggested something different, "though not necessarily something contradictory": the closeness of Canadian-American interests due to geographic proximity. He analyzed certain aspects of the agreement, including its evident acceptance by the public, despite Canada's long history of anti-American feeling, and its having taken the form of an executive agreement, rather than a formal treaty. The thing was, it seemed that "we in Canada are now committed to two loyalties, the old one to the British connection involving our backing up of Britain, and the new one to North America, involving common action with the States" to protect continental security. Not long ago, he said, discussion of such a realignment would have elicited accusations of disloyalty. Why was it welcomed now with such unanimous approval?[12]

Little did he know. His remarks were reported the next day in the *Orillia Packet and Times*, by now his seeming nemesis, and the Toronto *Telegram*, highlighting certain phrases he had used in answer to his question: "we can no longer put all our eggs in the British basket," and "the nineteenth century world under British economic leadership and kept peaceful by British sea-power has passed away forever." Cody began fielding calls from people who had read the press reports, if not from those who had actually heard the talk. He demanded that Underhill provide him a full statement of his remarks, which led to Underhill's written version. Members of the board of governors, including Chancellor Mulock, demanded an investigation. Former prime minister, now senator, Arthur Meighen wrote the federal justice minister, calling for Underhill's internment. A police investigation, undertaken at the request of the Ontario minister of education, found that Underhill had said nothing to warrant any action under the Defence of Canada Regulations. In an interview with Cody prior to the board of governors meeting of 12 September, Underhill demanded that the president show him anything in his talk that was disloyal or improper. He was genuinely surprised by the furore. The problem, Cody replied, was not with specific things he had said, but with his "constant making trouble for the University."[13]

For all the complications that unfolded over the next six months, amid increasing tensions, and pressures exerted both for and against Underhill's dismissal, this was the nub of the issue for President Cody. At first, the board decided not to take action, based partly on advice from the university's legal counsel, who recommended caution in the absence of clear documentary evidence, and partly because of support Underhill was able to muster from influential friends. He finished out the month of September with a sense of relief, though he told Scott it had been "the nastiest business" he had yet been through.[14] Demands for his termination continued to be made in the press and behind the scenes, however, and in December Cody decided to recommend in favour. Underhill was called to appear before a committee of the board on 2 January 1941, where he was offered the alternatives of voluntary resignation or dismissal. Resignation would supposedly afford him the opportunity to find another job, an opportunity he regarded as empty, since everyone would know the reasons for his resignation. He refused to resign, noting that he had been given no reason for doing so, other than the pressures of "public opinion," nor had he been charged with a specific offense.[15]

There followed a dramatic period of several weeks, during which students petitioned in Underhill's defence, senior colleagues met with the president to plead his case (again notably including Innis, who, a Great War veteran himself, put forward Underhill's wartime service in mitigation of his conduct), and numerous others wrote from across the country and the United States. Carleton Stanley, now president of Dalhousie University, acknowledged his friend's capacity to irritate but threatened to publicly resign both his undergraduate degree and his honorary Doctor of Laws if Underhill were fired.[16] Hugh Keenleyside, a senior official of the Department of External Affairs and Canadian secretary of the new Permanent Joint Board of Defence, went into action, writing the prime minister to urge his intervention, on the grounds that a dismissal could very well damage Canadian-American relations, and communicating with Cody and others to the same effect. The historian J.B. Brebner, who had been a member of the Toronto history department in the early 1920s, and who had been at Couchiching, wrote similarly from his position at Columbia. Time and again, Cody responded that the issue was not academic freedom, but the "recklessness" of Underhill's speech, his "serious defects of personality," and the disrepute he brought on the university.[17] On top of all the correspondence Cody received, newspapers across the country commented unfavourably on the infringement of Underhill's freedom of speech, which suggests (ironically) that the board's actions had probably damaged the reputation of the university, outside certain Toronto circles, more than quiet tolerance – or even noisy tolerance – would have done.[18]

As in all such matters, the most important interventions were rarely spontaneous. Underhill himself desperately canvassed friends for their support, including Keenleyside. These friends spoke to other friends. In Montreal, Scott did what he could to marshal support, including obtaining information about whether and how the American Association of University Professors might be brought in to assist. Donald Creighton, on sabbatical leave in Washington, wrote Scott to report on advice he had obtained from an official at the A A U P regarding the procedures to be followed.[19] Finally, and perhaps decisively, even Premier Hepburn advised against dismissal, prompted by word from a friendly colleague in Ottawa – who in turn had been prompted by J.W. Pickersgill and Brooke Claxton – warning of potential negative consequences for US relations and possibly American tourism. Cody and the board were forced reluctantly to back down. As late as June, a majority of board members were keen to move forward, but Cody, whose recommendation was required on all personnel matters, withdrew his recommendation for dismissal.[20]

The Underhill Affair – or *L'affaire Underhill*, as Frank Scott wryly referred to it, evoking *L'affaire Dreyfus* – gained a prominent place in the history of academic freedom in Canada, though it did little to formalize a definition of the concept or extend its protection. That was to come later, as a result of the attempted dismissal of another historian, Harry Crowe, from United College in Winnipeg in 1958 – the Crowe Affair. The real significance of the Underhill Affair was personal. He was back in touch with Scott in January, asking him (as he also had in September) to keep his ears open for job vacancies. He asked the same of Percy Corbett, relaying to both of them his concern for the effects of the crisis on his wife and daughter and his deep gratitude to his students and friends, as well as staff at the university and people beyond whom he did not even know, for their support.[21] The ulcer condition he had developed in the late thirties worsened. In September he had promised Cody to refrain from making public speeches outside the university for a year, an undertaking that he admitted to a friend was "unheroic" of him, but he was "past fifty years of age."[22] Unheroic, indeed. These were humiliating words for a man to whom intellectuals were heroes by definition. The whole experience was emotionally traumatic.

———————

Intellectually, however, it was the war itself more than his conflict with Cody and the university board of governors that led Underhill to follow his own advice, tendered earlier to historians, and reexamine his values and beliefs. He had begun to do so before the university crisis, with the renewal of war in Europe. At the beginning of September 1939, in the few days between the British and French declarations of war on Germany and Canada's formal decision to participate – "Parliament will decide," the prime minister had promised – he attended special meetings of the L S R executive in Montreal and the C C F national council in Ottawa. Both bodies were divided between those who favoured intervention and those who opposed, though there were nuances and differences on either side, and both bodies sought ways of papering over the disagreements. The L S R requested a clarification of war aims from the government and assurances of the protection of civil liberties, while the C C F declared its opposition to the sending of an expeditionary force overseas and its support only of economic aid to Britain. At the same time, it too expressed concern for civil liberties. J.S. Woodsworth was opposed to any participation at all, a position supported by others, including Underhill and Frank Scott.[23] The decision, however, was out of their control. Days later, Parliament adopted an address in reply to the speech from the throne that was unmistakable in approving Canada's entry into the war, even if it was ambiguous in detail. During a perfunctory debate, Woodsworth alone spoke in opposition, expressly out of step with his own party. There was no recorded vote.

Though it was not at all clear in the autumn of 1939 exactly what participation would entail, it was evident that Underhill's worst fears of the 1930s had come to pass. Canada had become a participant in another European war, and had done so (it seemed to him) more by virtue of its imperial tie to Britain than as the result of a purposeful independent choice, whatever the prime minister claimed about Parliament deciding. The challenge he now faced was to respond to new circumstances while maintaining some measure of consistency with his previous position. The problem was complicated by open disagreement with his friends and associates. Eric Havelock showed his unreserved support of participation in the war by resigning as treasurer of the *Canadian Forum*, recalling many years later that he could "no longer stomach its isolationism," a clear reference to Underhill.[24] Joe Parkinson also favoured full participation and joined Havelock in leaving the editorial board. At the same time, fear of reprisals led to the removal of the names of all editorial contributors from the journal's masthead, including Underhill's and George Grube's, whose vulnerability to political attack had also been demonstrated. The only names remaining were those of Eleanor Godfrey, now managing editor, and Louis A. Morris, the business manager.[25]

Underhill tried to define a new position by following up on the LSR executive's letter to the prime minister, which he had drafted. In an essay he wrote for the October issue of the *Forum*, he questioned the purposes of the war. What was it intended to achieve? If it was to stop Hitler and Germany, what about remedying the underlying conditions that had brought Hitler to power in the first place? No one was demanding answers to such questions, he complained, much less was anyone demanding a statement of "peace aims" from their government. The last war had ended with a reorganization of Europe, but one that had left various national minorities in various nation states, in the protection of whom the League had failed miserably, resulting in the escalation of "racial hatreds." A long-term solution to the internecine strife of European nations ought surely to be among the peace aims, perhaps an "economic United States of Europe" that might make possible a coordinated response to another depression, since the one just passed had helped to sharpen hatreds. Perhaps, more broadly, some international organization – "the next League of Nations" – ought to be constituted to provide for economic planning and cooperation as well as for political discussion, which so often proved fruitless, and structured in such a way as to prevent domination by the great powers.[26]

There was a further shift in the tone and substance of his writing early in the following year, when he took part in a series of lectures at the university that were later published under the auspices of the Canadian Institute of International Affairs. Taking as his subject "Canada and the Last War," he addressed Canada's relation to Britain as well as its military role in the war. Compared to his essay on foreign policy in *Social Planning for Canada*, his discussion of imperial relations was remarkably sober and his judgments practical and restrained. In the earlier essay he had praised Laurier for having charted a path to national autonomy, though he had also stressed that neither "national aloofness" nor a "pacifist spirit" had saved the Liberal leader from being swept up by the forces of imperialism. He had concluded then that it was necessary to understand war as an inherent part of capitalist civilization that would only be averted by "a world-wide reconstruction of our social and economic institutions." Now, in 1940, he was more ready to concede that Borden's demands for full consultation in imperial decision-making might have been the more effective policy, even if it had not been sustained after the war.[27] In part, Underhill may have been persuaded by the evidence he found in Borden's recently published memoirs, but the failure of Mackenzie King, Laurier's autonomist heir, to move Canada forward from essentially the same position it had occupied in 1914 was at least equally important. Either way, he didn't mention social reconstruction. Moreover, in both parts of his lecture he presented a cautionary review of the conscription crisis of the Great War and its impact on French-English relations, the lessons of which assumed the fact of war. He had not ceased to be a socialist, but he had ceased to offer a socialist analysis of the war.

It was true that he had promised Cody a year earlier to behave more reasonably, and that a university lecture series was different from a book elaborating an explicitly radical program, but it seems more likely that Underhill's new tone derived from his own realism. The declaration of war had changed everything, even if relatively little occurred in the opening months, in the so-called phony war. Then, in May 1940 Germany invaded Belgium, the Netherlands, Luxembourg, and France, leading to Dunkirk and France's surrender. The threat of a fascist conquest of western Europe, including Britain, became credible for the first time. One could no longer regard the war as just another conflict between capitalist powers. It was ironic, therefore, that the most serious clash he ever had with university authorities came in the following summer, after he had modified his judgment of the war considerably. While it was perhaps not surprising that his enemies should have taken his assessment of the Ogdensburg Agreement as merely an extension of his North American isolationism, it was just as much a response to the changing balance of power. A strong dose of idealism had always lain back of his Benthamite "hard realistic temper," but there was little opportunity now for it to show itself.

In the spring of 1941, after things settled down at the university, he tried to free himself of some of his commitments.

He asked Scott if he would assume responsibility for political commentary in the *Forum*. He himself was "awfully tired" of producing editorials and articles every month; besides, he was depressed by the war and had lost his urge to write. He also wondered if the LSR had not outlived its usefulness. Attendance at meetings had fallen away and branches beyond Toronto and Montreal seemed to be more or less moribund. Scott declined to do more on the *Forum*, pleading the excuse of his own work, but he agreed that the LSR seemed to have lost its steam. Perhaps some smaller group, more focused on research, might take its place, as Underhill had suggested.[28] Within a year, the LSR died away without formally disbanding, and without any organized successor. Interest had declined, partly because some members, like Havelock and Parkinson, disagreed with the leadership's ambivalence toward the war (though Havelock had been persuaded to stay on the executive), and partly because a revived CCF absorbed the energies of many who had been active before.[29]

Among the reasons Underhill offered Scott for wanting out of the *Forum* was that he had been neglecting his "book on Blake" – a major research project he had begun a few years earlier on Edward Blake, the nineteenth-century Liberal leader – and the demands of writing on current affairs were a serious, even potentially fatal, distraction. Later in the year, he decided to apply for a Guggenheim Fellowship, which would enable him to spend a year somewhere in the United States, providing him continuous time for research and taking him away from Toronto and the obligations that filled his time there. Those obligations, it must be said, were not so onerous that he refrained from participating in the electoral campaign of Joseph Noseworthy, the CCF candidate chosen to oppose Arthur Meighen, former prime minister and putative next leader of the Conservative party, in a by-election in York South in February 1942. He wrote Noseworthy's speeches and was elated by his candidate's surprise victory, one indication among others of the revival of CCF fortunes.[30] A month later, Underhill learned that his Guggenheim application had been successful, for a term of one year beginning the following September. He decided he would take up the fellowship at Columbia University in New York. Under the circumstances, a foreign city must have seemed a natural refuge.

———————

Underhill embarked on his Blake project in the late 1930s because he considered Blake a thinking man's Liberal whose ideas might throw some light on the Canadian liberal tradition, and whose career might illuminate the Liberal party's transition from a party of principle, as it had been under George Brown, to a party of interests, as it became under Laurier. In the space of two years, 1938 to 1939, he published four articles on different aspects of Blake's political thought and practice. One of these was a study of his role in the attempt to do away with appeals to the Judicial Committee of the Privy Council, the highest court in the British Empire, when he was federal minister of justice from 1875 to 1877; another told the story of his opposition to the Liberal party's adoption of the policy of "Unrestricted Reciprocity" in the election of 1891; a third examined his relations with Laurier in the period from 1882 to 1891, when first Blake (to 1887), and then Laurier, was party leader; and a fourth discussed Blake's "liberal nationalism" over the course of his career.[31] In addition, Underhill presented a paper to the CHA in 1942 on Reform ideas in the decade after Confederation, and wrote a second article on Blake's and Laurier's personal and political relations.[32] They all served as a means of working out his thinking about the present, as well as the past, as did just about everything he wrote, and like all his studies of men he admired, they occasionally revealed an identification of author and subject. Blake was someone about whom he thought far too little was known.

Part of Blake's appeal lay in his early association with Goldwin Smith and the Canada First movement just after Confederation, when journals like the *Canadian Monthly and National Review* and the *Nation*, Canada First's own outlet, speculated about his possible leadership of a new party. In a widely reported speech delivered in Aurora, Ontario, in October 1874, Blake called for a series of electoral reforms that would carry forward the democratic program of the early Clear Grits: compulsory voting, proportional representation, the secret ballot, and extension of the franchise. He also spoke in favour of Senate reform and declared his opposition to spending large amounts of money on pushing a Pacific railway through the Rocky Mountains, even if it meant that British Columbia might secede from the union in protest against the violation of the terms on which it had joined three years before. As if that were not enough, he condemned the practice of buying the loyalty of provinces by promises of federal largesse and called instead for the cultivation of a "national spirit," and for Canada to take control of its foreign relations by demanding a share in imperial decision-making through a form of imperial federation. Without such control, it might find itself "plunged into the horrors of war" by the policies of England. In light of the talk of a new party, and of Blake's resignation from the federal Liberal cabinet of Alexander Mackenzie earlier in the year, his speech seemed to many a declaration of independence. "For a time in the 1870's," wrote Underhill, "it seemed as if a new advanced school of thought was about to emerge from the Reform ranks" and break off, as the Grits had divided from "the Baldwin Reformers" in the early 1850s.[33] For various reasons, Blake's personality among them, that was not to happen, though more resignations and threats of resignation were to follow in the future.

Blake's program was doomed, Underhill argued, because Canadians were much less disposed to attach their national feelings to the intangible satisfactions of the spirit than to the material benefits of the Macdonald system. To these latter vulgar baubles, he said, Blake reacted with "the fastidious dislike of the highly educated professional man," a characterization that surely resonated personally. He was also "temperamentally pessimistic," another resonant phrase, which left him open to accusations that he had no faith in the future of the country.[34] Not least of his problems, he was seldom at ease, even among his followers, and had no political guile. Yet, though he failed to become prime minister, he was, in Underhill's judgment, "the outstanding Canadian Liberal" of the first generation of Confederation. He understood the significance of the achievement of responsible government as the basis of "a progressive extension of the range of self-government" as Canada matured. Underhill had reservations about what this meant for strengthening the jurisdiction of the provinces under the banner of "provincial rights," which seemed to him in contradiction with the nurturing of a "national spirit," but he conceded the importance of localism for Blake's generation. He had no reservations about its meaning for national autonomy, and he applauded Blake's opposition to colonial office attempts to supervise Canadian affairs and his efforts to expand Canada's treaty-making powers, which represented, he thought, "the very quintessence of Canadian Liberalism."[35]

Blake was a man of principle, above all, but he was also capable of changing his mind. In a masterful dissection of the issues involved in negotiations with Britain over the fate of the Supreme Court Act of 1875, one clause of which limited appeals to the Privy Council, Underhill showed how Blake stiffened the resolve of his cabinet colleagues in confronting officials in London, who were threatening disallowance, but was also persuaded that the wording of the offending clause had the effect of preserving the very right of appeal that it purported to abolish. The act was allowed to stand as it was, on the understanding that the clause became a dead letter. In response, Blake laid down a plan to return to the question in the near future, putting on record arguments for repeal that

Underhill noted were still being made in the 1930s, but illness – one of many bouts of what was known at the time as neurasthenia – led to his resignation.[36] On another front, in establishing a close working relationship with Laurier, Blake sought successfully to bridge the French-English divide that had plagued Reform ever since Macdonald had transformed Baldwin-Lafontaine Reform into the Liberal-Conservative party (with an assist from Sir Francis Hincks). Underhill's interest in this was a reflection of his growing recognition of the central importance of French-English relations in national politics and the shedding of his own Brownite attitudes toward French Canada.[37]

In this respect, Blake helped to lay the foundation of the modern Liberal party and, in so doing, to join with Laurier in moving the party away from its Grit roots. Similarly, his opposition to the policy of Unrestricted Reciprocity foreshadowed the party's reconciliation with protectionism, which paved the way for its return to office in 1896. Blake declared his opposition in a letter to his constituents in the riding of Durham West, in effect explaining his decision not to contest the election of 1891, but did so the day after the election, Laurier and others having persuaded him that publishing the letter any earlier would jeopardize the party's electoral prospects. Like his Aurora speech, the "West Durham letter" was widely circulated in the press and in pamphlet form, and generated vigorous debate. Blake had long thought that free trade – another staple of traditional liberalism – was not a viable policy, since the government required tariff revenues to support its expenditures. The question was not whether there were tariffs, but how high they needed to be to accomplish those ends. As for reciprocity with the United States, there was little hope that the Americans would agree, and a serious danger that, in "unrestricted" form, it would lead inexorably to political union. There could hardly have been a more damning condemnation of his own party's stated policy, and many of his colleagues and the party press condemned Blake in return.[38]

Underhill disputed the contention of previous authors that
the West Durham letter resulted in permanently strained relations between Blake and Laurier. Quoting at length from their
correspondence, he showed that, despite an interruption in
the months immediately after the election, it resumed on a
cordial basis, in pursuit of some means of reconciling their
differences. Blake denied that he actually favoured the
American union that he had warned of, as the *Globe* had
accused him of doing, writing a heartfelt affirmation of his
hopes for Canada that Underhill described as a "magnificent
peroration" to a document that was never published: "I cling
to the hope," Blake wrote, "of a higher though more arduous
destiny for the great Dominion." Laurier, consulting with
close colleagues of them both, insisted that Unrestricted
Reciprocity was not meant to be taken literally, but as an
aspiration for freer trade, an explanation that Blake could not
accept. The two men failed to come to an agreement and,
when an invitation came from the Irish Nationalists in the
British House of Commons to join their party and serve the
cause of Home Rule, he accepted. The Liberals' abandonment
of "U.R." after his departure and their adoption of a new policy of moderate protection, Underhill concluded, was a tacit
admission that Blake had been right, after all.[39] The fact that
the two leaders continued to correspond for the remainder of
Blake's life only confirmed Underhill's admiration for Blake's
ability to keep policy and personality separate. In a career of
active and recurring dissent, he represented for Underhill a
kind of surrogate third party on the nineteenth-century
national stage, in a time when no such party existed in reality.
He seemed an ideal subject for a larger-scale study.

Instead of devoting his Guggenheim year to Blake, however,
Underhill spent much of his time away catching up on his
reading in American history and politics, which led him to
begin thinking anew about third parties. The biography seems

to have taken second place, an early sign of his difficulties with the complexities and contradictions of his subject. The effects of his reading were apparent in a paper he gave at a meeting of the Canadian Political Science Association (C P S A), held in May 1943, on "The Canadian Party System in Transition." Only the year before, he had opened his C H A paper on post-Confederation Reform by citing Goldwin Smith's dictum that "party without principles inevitably becomes faction; and faction as inevitably supports itself by intrigue, demagogism and corruption."⁴⁰ Now, he had come to appreciate some of the virtues of the brokerage party model he had so often criticized in the past. Drawing, he said, on an American literature on parties that was far richer than anything in Canada, and that provided categories for study as applicable north of the border as south, he emphasized especially the way brokerage parties mitigated potentially destructive social divisions by finding common ground among divergent groups. In fact, he put forward the proposition that a democracy was "simply a society in which all interest groups have an equal chance to present their claims for benefits from the gains of civilization and to get them adjusted."⁴¹ In doing so, he seemed to be abandoning a socialist analysis of political parties, as he had earlier of war.

Still, he was not prepared to give up on parties as vehicles of ideas, even if their effectiveness in a democracy depended on their willingness to compromise, or on parties as expressions of class interests. "The rich want freedom, the poor want ham and eggs," he quoted from an unknown aphoristic source. He suggested, nonetheless, that the closer a party came to winning power, the more North American in character it would become. The main thesis of his paper, he said, having been asked to speak about Canadian political parties "in our contemporary crisis of democracy," was that in the past twenty years – that is, since the rise of the Progressives after the First World War – politics in Canada had been undergoing a transition from the old two-party system to a "new and more effective one." He thought it was likely that in the not-too-distant future a new political alignment would emerge, with the Liberals on the right, plus a remnant of Conservatives, whose difficulties in Quebec and western Canada seemed insuperable, and the CCF on the left. The CCF's rise to such a position, however, depended on its assimilation of the lessons of Canadian political history, including the need for a "bi-racial" coalition and a "positive national policy," which together had formed the basis of Conservative success under Macdonald, and Liberal success under Laurier. It also depended on the party's recognition of socialism, not as a "Platonic" abstraction but as a program attuned to the essential political question of "who gets what, when, where, and how." In the United States, he noted finally, no such realignment would occur because the Democrats had already shifted leftward in their sponsorship of the New Deal.[42] This distinguished Canada from the US, but it also left open the question of how the Democrats had managed it.

He was to continue his rethinking of parties, but for the moment, that was not the only thing that seemed to change during the months he spent at Columbia and, later, at Dartmouth College in Hanover, New Hampshire. In allowing him to see things in a fresh light when he returned, his time away may have had as much influence on his self-examination as the university crisis that had led to it, though even yet the impact was more subtle than dramatic in its external manifestations. In May 1943, just before he came home briefly to attend the CPSA meetings, he received a letter from Carlton McNaught, who was minding the editorial side of things at the *Forum*, enclosing a "disturbing" letter from Harry Cassidy, in which their former colleague argued for the merits of a "mixed economy." Not only would it avoid inevitable administrative problems that would arise if all businesses were socialized, Cassidy thought, but "the evidence of recent years" led him to wonder if political democracy could survive "when all economic power [was] under the control of the state." This seemed to McNaught a betrayal of socialist principles: "New Dealism" was not enough.

He must have been surprised to get a reply back from Underhill (and perhaps later to read his friend's c p s a paper as well) agreeing with Cassidy. At the very least, Underhill wrote, any socialist electoral victory would be followed by a transitional period in which government would have to cooperate with business – or some businesses – in achieving its ends, but he also shared Cassidy's worries about freedom in a situation where the state was "the nearly universal employer." He added that he thought it behoved the Ontario c c f to begin planning for particular actions, including changes to education and health care, rather than "worrying over abstract socialism," which risked appealing only to the doctrinaire.[43] Three months later, attending a celebration of c c f gains in the provincial election of 4 August, when the party had won 34 seats (placing it second to the Conservatives in a minority legislature), he was put off by the temper of the celebrants, who seemed to revel in the triumph of the "forces of light over darkness." This seemed to him, he later recalled, "inherently insincere."[44]

One may wonder if the celebrations were all that different from those following Noseworthy's victory, but perhaps the c c f had changed as well. Many of its activists now smelled power, and Underhill's view of the party had always been that it served an educational (or "missionary") purpose, to disseminate proposals for change and generate debate that would lead to their implementation. Those who pursued power made him uncomfortable, as if they were not really very different from the Macdonalds and Lauriers and Mackenzie Kings. His fears seemed to be confirmed by the pressures that leading members of the c c f – especially the national secretary, David Lewis, but also George Grube, who had become a party official – began to put on the *Forum* to support the party both editorially and in its articles. Underhill inevitably became a target of their criticisms, even though, in the view of Eleanor Godfrey, it was "F.H.U." who gave the journal "what distinction it has."[45] He was not one to conform to any orthodoxy. It did not help that his strongest personal bond to the party had been severed in March 1942, with the death of Woodsworth, the personification of the missionary conception of the party. When he spoke at the inauguration of the Woodsworth Memorial Foundation in October 1944, he said he hoped that the CCF would remain a movement for social and economic change, as Woodsworth had thought of it, and not sink into "being merely a party intent on collecting votes."[46] He had criticized Woodsworth himself, of course, for organizational deficiencies, but the danger of politics was that, in pursuing victory, one might become intent on achieving it over one's friends as well as one's adversaries, and lose sight of what victory was for. Woodsworth had never been guilty of that.

Underhill's demands for CCF self-criticism grew more forceful the more he came to believe that the "contemporary crisis of democracy" to which he made passing reference in his CPSA paper surpassed all other issues in importance. In January 1945, he returned to his early hero, John Morley, in a lecture delivered at the University of Toronto. Reading it today, one marvels at its sheer length – thirty-eight handwritten pages – and density. In many ways it was characteristic of his style and method: superficially, in its cramped handwriting, replete with the shorthand symbols he had used ever since his undergraduate years; more revealingly, in the pages and pages of notes on Morley's books and essays, and on works about Morley that formed the basis of his discussion, as similar notes preserved in his personal papers demonstrate the concentration of his reading on all subjects; and most suggestively, in the lecture's dialogic relation with the past and its attempt to communicate a long-forgotten message to the present. It was an exercise in retrieval, like his essays on Blake and Smith, and functioned as a vehicle for registering the evolution of his own thought. The last of these seemed to carry more weight than usual, a hint of some larger intellectual change in progress.

He began in a familiar way, recalling his early admiration for Morley, and went on to outline for his audience his subject's varied career: a journalist, editor successively of the *Edinburgh Review* and the *Pall Mall Gazette*; a politician, serving terms in Liberal cabinets as chief secretary for Ireland and secretary of state for India; and an author of biographies of Voltaire, Rousseau, Burke and others, as well as of Gladstone, in addition to countless essays. Though a "minor" figure, he had been a typical "Victorian liberal agnostic" who believed in human rationality and the innate goodness of human nature. This was an outlook, Underhill thought, that was only too likely to be mocked in the present day: "For are we not living in an age of religion again, and are we not assured by our best religious thinkers that man is a poor sinful creature needing grace from some supernatural source for his redemption? And are we not told by our psychologists and psychiatrists that man's reason is the helpless sport of his unconscious self, and that men in the mass are mere dupes destined to be manipulated and exploited by a Machiavellian elite of realists who know that power is all that matters in the world?" He was now less comfortable with such views, he seemed to be saying, than he had been when they had come from modern, secular men like Walter Lippmann and Graham Wallas.

Morley's works on eighteenth-century France had been especially interesting for their attempt to rescue the reputation of the *philosophes* from the pall cast over it by the mysticism of earlier writers such as Thomas Carlyle. To modern eyes, accustomed to the clarity and verve of Carl Becker's *The Heavenly City of the Eighteenth-Century Philosophers* (1932), "that unique paragon of all modern works of historical criticism," Morley's French studies inevitably seemed "ponderous" and "moralizing," but they had made abstract ideas accessible to ordinary readers and reminded them of the foundations of the liberalism of their own day. Morley had thought that day to be the dawn of a new age, whereas, on the contrary, it had marked the beginning of the end of liberalism, of which no better evidence could be found than the fate of Home Rule for Ireland, the rise of imperialism, and the failure of British policy in India. The Fabians had been the real heirs of "the Benthamite liberal tradition," not Morley's Liberals. He personally had been strongly opposed to any state intervention in the economy, yet his awareness of the roots of radicalism contained lessons for the present day, when it was necessary "to find our way back to that faith which uplifted men in the age of reason. We shall have to rediscover the truth," Underhill concluded, "that the most important fact about man is that he is a rational creature."[47] It was not clear that Underhill had yet found his own way back to that faith, but there was no doubting the urgency of his summons.

He repeated the language of crisis in his presidential address to the CHA the following year, in which he lamented the failure of Canadians to contribute anything significant to the debate that was consuming the current generation elsewhere, involving "those deep underlying intellectual, moral and spiritual issues which have made such a chaos of the contemporary world," and which concerned, above all, "the fundamental values of liberalism and democracy." They seemed to have nothing to say about the "modern crisis of liberalism," whose origins reached back into the nineteenth century, when the optimistic liberal nationalism of the early century had mutated into the *realpolitik* conservative nationalism of the later, and on to the totalitarianism of the twentieth.[48] He had alluded to this problem of silence five years earlier at another meeting of the CHA, in calling on academics to involve themselves in the "deep social and cultural struggle of their time" and defend the "tradition of rational free inquiry."[49] His call for involvement was nothing new – the fact that he had been elected to the highest office in his profession reflected the esteem in which he was held by his colleagues, whatever criticisms he had made of them over the years – but the terms of struggle were undergoing a tectonic shift because of the war and the geopolitical conflicts arising from it.

Canadians had achieved many things, he told his audience, and had made great sacrifices in two world wars fought in defence of democracy within a single generation, but they remained a colonial people in the realm of ideas, dependent on thinkers in London, New York, Paris, and elsewhere for their "intellectual capital." This included – "incidentally," as if to remind his audience of his customary role – in the field of history, where, with few exceptions, Canadians had contributed little to the advancement of knowledge of societies beyond their borders. Even in the study of their own society, they depended on outsiders – such men as Goldwin Smith, André Siegfried, J.A. Hobson, and James Bryce – for insightful analysis, never managing themselves to bring ideas to "an articulate life of their own." The constant theme of those analyses by outsiders was "the poverty of our politics at the intellectual level." The contrast with the United States, which had produced a generation of major thinkers at the time of the republic's founding, despite being a collection of small frontier communities, could not be sharper. The reason, he thought, lay in the weakness of Canada's radical tradition, which in turn was the result of both English and French Canada, for different reasons, having rejected the eighteenth-century Enlightenment. This had somehow become a cause of celebration, and movements for democratic reform, to the extent that their proposals seemed American in origin, were tarred with an anti-American brush, inhibiting intellectual exchange and advance. He suggested that historians were not entirely blameless here, either, and called for a new intellectual history that would uncover what Canadians had been thinking in the past and show what place they had in the "civilization of the liberal-democratic century" that lay behind them.[50]

Another part of the explanation for the weakness of the radical tradition, he now thought, was that Canadian radical movements had been "too purely agrarian," and farmers in the countryside were less able to understand the power of urban business than were the "democratic labour movements in the big cities and their sympathizers amongst the urban intellectuals." He had come to this conclusion after reading Arthur M. Schlesinger Jr's *The Age of Jackson* (1945), which he (and many others) considered a "brilliant" reinterpretation of the movement that had brought US president Andrew Jackson to office, locating its origins in the new industrial cities rather than on the western frontier, from where it had previously been thought to emanate. This was the best and worst of Underhill. He enlivened historical debate with new insights but managed to imply in the process that everyone else was a bit dull and backward in failing to come to them as promptly as he had. His reading of Schlesinger, in any case, had led him to a new understanding of why the Clear Grit and *Rouges* movements had led nowhere: responsible government, that supposed icon of Canadian liberalism, had absorbed and reoriented North American democratic energies in a British Whig direction. George Brown, he had now come to see, became more a "business man on the make" than an agrarian democrat as he grew older, representing interests that radical liberals necessarily opposed, while his beloved Blake – whom he now described as "leader of the Ontario equity bar" – was more an English Whig than a democrat in temperament, training, and political philosophy, little moved by the ideal of economic equality. One can almost sense his enthusiasm for his biographical subject wither on the page.[51]

––––––––––––

Underhill's reconception of what was at stake in the contemporary world had political, as well as historical, implications, which soon became evident in his *Forum* pieces and his relations with CCF colleagues. Far from being anomalies in the modern world – embodiments of evil – Nazi Germany and Communist Russia were forms of government, he thought, to which any people might succumb if they were not careful to limit the power of the state. Socialist movements, which sought to expand the state, needed to be especially mindful of the dangers. This was why it was essential, he wrote in the *Forum* in 1947, for CCFers to remember that their party had been created with the ultimate goal of emancipating ordinary men and women from "the most oppressive tyranny of all – the economic regimentation and degradation that are caused by poverty, unemployment, and insecurity." They must not allow "planning" to become a mystical incantation, as "free enterprise" had become for capitalists; the question was, how to mix planning and free enterprise. Theirs, in others words, was a liberal socialism, the implementation of which would require all the "imagination, initiative and vision" that had marked the early days of capitalism. He especially warned them of the pitfalls of the term "Soviet democracy," which he thought an oxymoron, and of somehow equating the iniquities of American capitalism with those of the Soviet state: "The real division of the world today," he declared, "is not between socialism and capitalism, it is between freedom and totalitarianism."[52] This was not a message all his comrades-in-arms were happy to hear.

Grube, for one, took to the pages of the *Forum* to protest that socialist planning and democratic liberty were both essential parts of democratic socialism. A socialist, he wrote, was opposed to both totalitarianism and capitalism: "If it is foolish (as it is) to accept or excuse the totalitarianism of the Soviet Union through hatred of capitalism, it is also foolish to blind oneself to the criminal wastes of American capitalism (less obvious though these are in a period of relative, if temporary, prosperity) through one's hatred of totalitarianism." Taking up Underhill's warnings about the need to maintain the independence of such institutions as churches, political parties, and unions – the latter two, especially, in potential danger of subordination to the state – he responded that, of course, excessive state power was a danger – what human activity was free of danger? – but there was nothing in socialism to threaten any of them. Employees of "the state," for example, would be employees of public corporations, not of government, and to the extent that government supervised them, it would be accountable to the people.[53] Grube's annoyance was fully evident, even if he lacked Underhill's rhetorical panache. Frank Scott wrote from Montreal, citing newspaper articles that welcomed Underhill's apparent recantation, objecting, as he had done before, to that very panache. If the article had been worded differently, the enemies of the CCF would not have been able to exploit it for their own ends.[54]

One positive response that Underhill received came in a long letter from an unexpected quarter, the Liberal-Progressive premier of Manitoba, Stuart Garson, whose coalition had soundly defeated the provincial CCF only two years before, on its way to re-election. The fact that he read the *Forum* at all is an indication of the journal's reach; that he wrote like this, out of the blue, is an indication of Underhill's. He wondered what it was that distinguished liberal Manitobans like himself, who supported government ownership of their telephone system, their hydro-electric system, and two radio stations, not to mention a public monopoly of liquor sales, from socialists. Surely "genuine socialism" of a Marxian variety extended state controls far beyond ownership of certain enterprises. He agreed that the "real division" of the present was between freedom and totalitarianism, but didn't that place both of them on the same side? If indeed it made them allies, he might not mind being called a liberal socialist, "but I think with deference that by a proper exercise of verbal definition it seems more likely that you are a liberal than I am a socialist."[55] Garson may not have been a socialist, but he was perceptive in detecting the underlying tensions in Underhill's assessment of the relationship of socialism and freedom, which may explain why Underhill did not reply.

Party allegiance was a different matter. Underhill was not about to break from the CCF, however much he was concerned about the party's vision of the role of the state, but the new age of democratic socialism that he had anticipated in his essay on Bentham in 1933 was now cast into doubt because the liberalism he had taken for granted as its basis was itself in need of defending. The war really had changed everything. It had shown that there was profound danger in state power itself, even more so when it was coupled with belief in an absolute good – belief, that is, that one was on the side of the forces of light – and with a program that was overly abstract. "The fox knows many things," the British intellectual historian Isaiah Berlin once famously wrote, quoting the Greek poet Archilochus, "but the hedgehog knows one big thing." Berlin was writing specifically about Leo Tolstoy, the greatest hedgehog of nineteenth-century European literature, but he suggested that thinkers in general could be divided between those "who pursue many ends," entertaining "ideas that are centrifugal rather than centripetal, their thought … scattered or diffused," and those "who relate everything to a single central vision" or "a single, universal organizing principle"; between pluralists, that is, and monists.[56] Underhill was irreducibly a fox in this sense, more disposed to ask questions – never satisfied, to the annoyance of some – than to offer all-embracing answers. It was only a matter of time before this led to conflict with his party.

In Search of Canadian Liberalism

Liberalism belongs to the left, or else it becomes meaningless.
F.H. Underhill, 1958

More than a decade passed before Stuart Garson's logic worked itself out in Underhill's own mind. Even then, he did not think of himself as abandoning his principles so much as moderating them and adopting a more practical means of putting some of them into practice in his own lifetime. In a warm and witty letter to Lester B. Pearson immediately after Pearson's election to the leadership of the Liberal party in January 1958, Underhill congratulated his old friend ("Dear Mike"), saying that he was the only person capable of turning the party in a "liberal [small-l] direction." He proceeded to tender advice, unasked. Pearson was not to follow the example of US president Dwight D. Eisenhower and pose as a friend "to the whole damned human race," but to use his wide party support to assert strong leadership and override factional differences. The party had failed in the past to educate either its followers or the public in general – which was the function of a political party – or to form a platform with any intellectual substance. Instead, it had become a party of expediency. Pearson needed to court the "great many intellectual and educated people" who might be attracted to liberalism, setting up "some sort of brain trust from university men" and holding summer conferences on the model of the Port Hope conference of 1933, when Vincent Massey had organized a meeting (at his own expense) to rethink policy. He had to recruit young, independent-minded members and, if possible, to parachute someone like Tom Kent, the thoughtful and knowledgeable editor of the *Winnipeg Free Press*, into the editorial chair of the *Globe and Mail* to educate public opinion in central Canada. Above all, he must not stick to the middle of the road: "Liberalism belongs to the left or else it becomes meaningless."[1] He needed to woo CCF voters and save his political salvos for those on the right. Mind you, Underhill concluded, he himself would be voting CCF in the next election.

Still resistant to actually supporting the Liberals, he seemed nevertheless ready to do so once the party came under new, more sympathetic leadership. Following his activities and the evolution of his ideas over the previous ten years, this does not come as a surprise, but Underhill's change of political allegiance was not simply an ideological mutation. It was also a response to a changing environment. His ideas about the role of the CCF, and the nature of parties in general, moved further in the direction they had begun to take in the early forties, as the CCF failed to fulfill his expectations of supplanting the Conservatives as the second of two main parties, suffering electoral losses nationally that left them with fewer seats in the House of Commons than they had won in 1945. He also came directly into conflict with senior members of the party over the role of the Woodsworth Memorial Foundation. His views on foreign policy underwent a change, but those on relations with the United States stayed much the same, only in neither case were they any longer the mark of radicalism that they had been in the 1930s. They had more to do with his continuing concern for the postwar crisis of liberalism.

In 1955, following his retirement from the University of Toronto, he moved to the more Liberal-friendly environs of Ottawa. These were not quite the same, however, as they had been a decade or so earlier. Liberal attitudes toward the role of the state had changed, under the influence of the Depression and the war, making it possible to think that the party just might become the vehicle of social and economic reform that he had once hoped for, obviating the need for a third party further to the left. It would be too much to say that everyone was a social democrat now, but social democracy moved into the mainstream.

A revealing index of Underhill's rethinking of the CCF and political parties can be found in his evolving assessment of Mackenzie King in the 1940s. During these years, he moved from a judgment of King's success as being the result of the pitiful weakness of his opponents, more than his own leadership qualities, to suggesting that it was actually more solidly based and carried lessons for his own party. Writing in the *Forum* in 1944, he was forced to acknowledge the prime minister's success but found it "hard not to snort," along with everyone else, when King claimed it was based on the principles set out in his 1918 book, *Industry and Humanity*. Lofty as those principles were – "uplifting abstract moral platitudes," Underhill called them in reviewing a new abridged edition of the book in 1948 – there was little to show for their implementation in the fields of labour relations, competition law, social services, or constitutional reform, while their author had done little to advance national autonomy. Apart from the ineptitude of his chief rival, the Conservatives, his string of election victories had been made possible by the preference of Canadians for living in a "mental haze." Two years later, Underhill's assessment was much the same, though he did express some chagrin at how often in the past the *Forum* – that is, he himself – had predicted King's imminent political demise, only to be proven wrong. Why had middle-class Liberal parties survived in North America, unlike in Europe, where they had been crushed between old Conservatives and new working-class movements, and why had

Canadian Liberals failed to respond to economic crisis as American Democrats had with the New Deal? History suggested that the answer lay in the defeat of the liberal democratic rebellions of 1837.[2]

Underhill greeted "the end of the King era" in August 1948 – King having resigned in February and just been succeeded by Louis St Laurent – with a rather different view of his career. Now his undoubted success was in bringing diverse interest groups together to arrive at a common policy, and in making them aware of "what they have in common rather than of what divides them," a rather more positive judgment than mere political manipulation. This was especially important in the area of French-English relations. Still holding him at a distance, Underhill described King as "the representative Canadian, the typical Canadian, the essential Canadian, the ideal Canadian, the Canadian as he exists in the mind of God." Yet there was no irony in his summing up of King's achievements in bringing the country out of the "halfway house" of Dominion status, to which Laurier and Borden had taken it (a judgment rather different from eight years earlier), in bringing it through the war "without precipitating an irreconcilable split between French and English Canadians," and in realizing that Canada could not manage in the twentieth-century world – nor could Britain, for that matter – "except in close co-operation with the United States." Then, squaring the circle, he concluded that King had not been very good at absorbing the demands – as distinct from putting them off – of organized agriculture and labour, failing in this respect to prepare the Liberal party for the new Canada. He had no constructive national policy. No one could predict which party would fill the role of Macdonald's Conservatives and Laurier's and King's Liberals in the future, but for the first time there was a "real chance" for creating the necessary "combination of anti-big-business groups" that would advance Canadian democracy and truly bring the King era to an end.[3]

In his last contribution to this series, written on the occasion of King's death in July 1950, Underhill acknowledged again that the *Forum* had "as unbroken a record of hostile criticism" of the late prime minister as any Canadian journal, but King had "defeated all his critics." Perhaps that called for some reflection, he wrote, by which he clearly meant some second thought. King had an "unparalleled intuitive capacity" for seeing what voters wanted, though his was not the kind of leadership welcomed by "the more intellectual elements of the community." They ("we") said he never gave a lead, but Canada was the kind of country resistant to precipitate action or strong speech. The one exception to his reluctance to lead was in external affairs, where he understood what Canadians wanted better than they did themselves, recognizing that their future lay in North American cooperation more than in the British Empire and Commonwealth. At the same time, he had managed to avoid provoking the usual anti-American backlash, except among those "academic intellectuals" who combined "nasty wisecracks" about American imperialism with acceptance of grants from the big American foundations. The lesson for the CCF was twofold: any party that aspired to govern Canada needed the consent and cooperation of French Canadians; more generally, it could not be a class party but had to bring together a "loosely knit collection of voters from all groups." The CCF and the Progressive party had been attempts to introduce a British structure of politics to Canada, with parties of the left and right, but King had defeated all such attempts with "a typical North American party." Underhill concluded that the CCF – "we C.C.F.ers" – ought to be "mature enough" to learn from King. Otherwise they would find their platform planks – the ones attractive to voters, at least – stolen by their rivals.[4]

He had come around to a sympathetic view of the "North American" party in the early 1940s, as we have seen, and, with it, to the virtues of the two-party system, but he was no longer so confident that the CCF would graduate to major-party status. The party had stood for the alternative British model, and its success would have represented the success of that model, even if it had taken his advice and accentuated the positive and the practical in its program. Now the North American model was even more compelling. In an essay on "Political Parties and Ideas" written for the Canadian volume of a United Nations series on member states in 1950, he blurred the line – which he had earlier drawn so sharply – between the British heritage of the Liberal and Conservative parties and the North American parties they had become in the course of the nineteenth century. Their leaders, he wrote, continued to quote their British counterparts, and the cabinet system "tended to impress" a British stamp on Canadian parties. In its representation of the British party model, then, the CCF's distinctiveness was slightly diminished, even if its democratic structure contrasted favourably with that of the Liberals and Conservatives. Its ambition had been to become the "second party," which would have given voters a choice between left and right, "socialists and anti-socialists," but this had proven "unrealistic." At the same time, all parties now professed to be "progressive," in favour of social security and "state regulation of the economy for the benefit of the masses." If a two-party system emerged in the future, he concluded, it might look very much like that of Macdonald and Laurier.[5]

Three years later, he followed this line of thinking to its conclusion. Writing in the *Forum* in July 1953 of the upcoming federal election, he expressed dismay at the prospects of the CCF. It had failed to become the second party and had "no real hope of being anything more than a splinter group," at least for the present. Mackenzie King had defeated its attempt to introduce "a British pattern" into Canadian politics. "The CCF's primary aim," Underhill went on, "was not to establish 'socialism' but to bring about a division between a party of the left and a party of the right like that between British Labour and Conservatives."[6] This was a decided shift of emphasis. For the purposes of the moment, his point was that, by fudging all issues and seeming to be all things to all people, King had managed to make the CCF seem a marginal movement of "impractical doctrinaires." The Liberals would probably win again, despite the threat that their arrogance posed to parliamentary democracy, because Canadians were still in the "state of trance" that he had induced, and because the Conservatives were no real alternative. In the longer term, Underhill seemed to be saying that the significance of the CCF lay in its party type more than in its socialism, from which it followed that its failure was less the failure of its program than its party model.

He may have been led to this conclusion partly because of the tensions that had developed between him and party leaders in the late forties and early fifties, parallel with his reassessment of Mackenzie King and political parties. Having participated in the inauguration of the Woodsworth Memorial Foundation in 1944, he joined in the founding of Ontario Woodsworth House on Jarvis Street in downtown Toronto, in a building purchased with funds raised by the foundation. Designed as an educational centre, the house contained meeting rooms and a small library, as well as additional space – it was a three-storey residence – plus a carriage house that was rented out to allied organizations, including the *Forum* and the Ontario CCF. As educational director, Underhill was in charge of organizing lectures, publishing pamphlets, and acquiring materials for the library. He thought of Woodsworth House as a kind of reembodiment of the LSR, which would operate independently of the CCF while at the same time contributing to the development of socialism in Canada by its educational activities, in this way building on the legacy of the man after whom it was named. What the CCF needed, he wrote in the course of a long two-part history of the Fabian Society, published in the *Forum*, was an equivalent organization (Woodsworth House not named) that would engage in research, discussion, and writing, "without being tied down to the official orthodoxy of any particular school of doctrine, or held in leash by the bureaucratic stupidity or the opportunist tactics of a political party machine," and so prevent a party's program from becoming "ossified and obsolete."[7] He was back in his take-no-prisoners mode.

As had always been the case, the tone in which he expressed his ideas about party and policy provoked negative reactions among some of his listeners and readers, if also positive ones among others. The ideas themselves, however, were no less contentious, as in his *Forum* essay warning of the dangers of statism that moved George Grube and Stuart Garson to respond. The essay had originated in a Woodsworth House lecture, where its impact had been no less divided.[8] By Underhill's lights, the controversy was a mark of success, though he was sometimes taken aback by the force of the reactions he aroused. In any event, he and others on the board of the foundation thought it best that Woodsworth House not be identified with any party, while party activists, David Lewis and Grube among them, thought of it as an arm of the CCF. The same issues that had already come up at the *Forum*, in other words, also came up at Woodsworth House, with many of the same people involved on either side, and Underhill at the centre.[9]

There was no shortage of party criticism in a lecture he delivered at the House in October 1950 to mark the fiftieth anniversary of the founding of the British Labour party, "Socialism after 50 Years." Reiterating that Woodsworth had been primarily an educator, and that Woodsworth House was likewise dedicated to education above all, he suggested that CCFers did not read enough, with the result that meetings descended into dreary repetition of the party's sacred texts, the Regina Manifesto and *Social Planning for Canada*. The changes wrought by the war, he said, called for new thinking. The party had been founded in an atmosphere still imbued with the nineteenth-century liberal ideals of liberty, equality, and fraternity, which socialism was to bring to fruition. Now they lived in an age when rationalism was under attack, when anxiety about renewed war and depression threatened an "escape from freedom" to authoritarianism (an idea first put forward by the emigré German psychologist and philosopher Erich Fromm in 1941), and when new technologies eased the transition from authoritarianism to totalitarianism. Under the circumstances, one of the first tasks of socialists was to identify new centres of power that would balance the growing power of the state. They also had to recognize the reality of power in modern international relations, the need for practical policies (like those of the Labour party) free of dogma, and the complexity of the middle classes (his plural) in modern society, from whose ranks the party needed to recruit members in order to expand its constituency. What was needed, in short, was more "modernists" and fewer "fundamentalists." Without fresh thinking, someone else – the Liberals being the obvious candidates – would invade their turf and come up with their own progressive policies for housing, health, education, and social services. He concluded – how else? – by handing out a reading list.[10]

He was not alone in thinking along these lines. When he started a newsletter in the fall of 1951, some members welcomed it, including the "jab in the arm" delivered by his critical comments, while others objected to his "ill-natured," persistent negativism.[11] In correspondence with M.J. Coldwell, who had succeeded Woodsworth as national CCF leader and with whom Underhill's relations were almost as close, the two of them concurred in their skepticism of "doctrinaire socialism," their admiration for G.D.H. Cole, a proponent of socialist education in Britain and a long-time member of the Fabian Society, and their belief in the need for renewal of the party. Too many people, Coldwell wrote on one occasion, thought of the Regina Manifesto "as the Word once delivered to the elect."[12] Yet Underhill's critics, Grube among them, did not think the educational efforts of Woodsworth House justified the time and money spent on supporting them, a claim that became more pointed as the foundation ran into financial difficulties maintaining the building.

The dispute over the purpose of Woodsworth House came to a head at the foundation's annual meeting in February 1952. The board of directors proposed to sell the Jarvis Street house and move into smaller quarters, where the focus would be on educational activities, and where there would be no surplus space for other organizations, such as the Ontario C C F. In their view, some of the responsibility for their financial troubles derived from the extremely low rent they received from the party. The sides that had been forming over the preceding months – that had existed, really, from the foundation's beginning – were out in force for the meeting. The "party" side, in fact – the side that resented criticisms levelled at the party and blamed the financial difficulties on the foundation's educational activities – was unusually strong. The president, in presenting his annual report, suggested that the meeting had been packed by new members who were showing an interest in Woodsworth House for the first time. As if to confirm his allegation, David Lewis moved an amendment to his report, affirming that the foundation ought to focus on building support for socialism among organizations such as cooperatives and trade unions, that the House should be a "home for the C.C.F. in Ontario," and that it should not be sold "without consent of the C.C.F. Ontario section."[13] The party side won, and a slate of new officers was elected, led by Lewis, though they did not defeat the incumbent board members entirely.

The conflict left the participants bitterly divided. Underhill's opponents later charged that he had not even attended the meeting, but he had been there, only too ill with another ulcer flare-up to speak.[14] He made his opinion known in the April issue of the *Forum*. The affair confirmed his view of Lewis as a party *apparatchik*: he had directed the drive for new members and the "purge" of the old board "with an unscrupulous thoroughness that the Communists themselves could hardly have bettered." Accustomed to giving direction in his office, he, and those like him, had little sympathy for the kind of people "who derive stimulation and amusement from letting their minds play with ideas and from asking inconvenient questions." A political party doubtless needed both paid bureaucrats and playful intellectuals, but the bureaucrats were congenitally prone to resent criticism and stamp out independence. This was a characterization of Lewis that Underhill would not revoke in the future. The congealment of ideas was an especially ominous weakness for the CCF in Ontario, he wrote, where support had been declining both federally and provincially, despite the fact that Ontario was the country's most urbanized province. Could they be sure that, instead of following the path blazed by Labour in Britain to major-party status, they would not suffer the fate of the American Socialist party, now a ghost of its former self? "Progressive, humanitarian, radical individuals" in the United States now supported the New Deal through various organizations, including the Democratic Party, preferring to see something actually accomplished to contemplating their own ideological purity.[15] If the party's prospects were to improve, it needed to engage in political education. Underhill's opponents, for their part, thought he was a Liberal in CCF clothing.

———————

Canada's external relations underwent a reorientation in the years following the war. The weakened position of Britain meant that it was no longer a reliable protector or the primary influence on policy, though it remained for many a focus of loyalty. The rise of the United States to great power status in a newly bipolar world meant that it would assume a more important position in international relations, whether Canadians liked it or not. Resentment of American power and influence grew, not only in rebellion against its inexorability, but also in a renewal of traditional anti-Americanism, which had reached its nadir at the time of the Ogdensburg Agreement.[16] Criticism of (and disdain for) American mass culture, and concern for America's imperial aspirations and their role in the beginnings of the Cold War gave it a new edge. The modernity the United States had once stood for lost its sheen. The term "Cold War" itself was a new one, coined by George Orwell and given currency in 1947 by Walter Lippmann.[17] Those who stood squarely with the United States were now seen as Cold Warriors. In these circumstances, Underhill's continuing continentalism, and his rejection of isolationism in favour of active alliance with the US, came under criticism from his intellectual and political allies on the left.

One close associate with whom he had a particularly sharp exchange was his student, Kenneth McNaught, whom he had known from childhood. McNaught finished his doctoral thesis on Woodsworth's early career, written under Underhill's supervision, in May 1950, and four months later published an essay in the *Forum* that took a decidedly critical view of his mentor's position on Canada's relations with the United States. He wrote it using the pseudonym S.W. Bradford, perhaps out of concern for offending Underhill, though in remembering it years later he could not recall his reason for adopting it. It made no difference, since Underhill learned who the author was before writing a blistering rebuttal in the next issue. "Bradford" contrasted the criticisms of American foreign policy mounted in the US itself, and in western Europe, with the "obeisance" of the Canadian government and the failure of the CCF to mount a critique of its own. In a gesture that can hardly have been made without his supervisor in mind, he invoked Edward Blake's West Durham letter in warning of a new Canadian colonial dependence on the United States. It cannot have helped that the article appeared in the same issue as Underhill's essay on the death of Mackenzie King, in which he referred to wisecracking academic intellectuals.[18]

He bristled in reaction. He called Bradford one of a number of "disgruntled CCF fundamentalists," unable to accept that Canada's freedom of manoeuvre had become severely constricted in a bipolar world. Citing specific actions of the United States and the Soviet Union, he demanded Bradford offer specifics in return, and propose concrete alternatives instead of "skilfully coloured suggestive statements" pitting American "devils" against "pure and uncorrupted Bradfordite socialists." Bradford warned of Canada becoming a satellite of the United States, while anyone who kept up with British intellectual journals would recognize that he himself was a satellite of Kingsley Martin's *New Statesman*, which had become a bastion of anti-Americanism in the UK. In fact, Underhill argued, most British socialists took a position much like the CCF, recognizing that the Soviet Union was unwilling to compromise on such issues as the atomic bomb, the future of Korea, and disarmament, and that, in a world that had shrunk, isolation from the struggle between the two world powers was not an option.

The mistake of the 1930s – and here Underhill added a footnote confessing that he had been "one of the foolish isolationists" of the time who had not believed reports of the strength of the German army and air force – had been to think that Europe could settle its internal conflicts without North American intervention. He might have been mistaken then, but at least he had learned the lesson that in a world dominated by power, one had to align oneself accordingly and temper one's belief in the efficacy of rational argument, however much one believed in its value. This might be difficult to accept, but the liberal nationalist traditions of the nineteenth century were simply no longer relevant. As for the idea that Canada's relation to the United States was similar to its colonial dependence on Britain sixty years earlier, it was "nonsense." There was nothing in the feelings Canadians had for the United States remotely comparable to their earlier emotional identification with the "mother-country," or to the cries of disloyalty that greeted anyone who questioned it.[19]

This was ostensibly a defence of the CCF, but it was one cast very much in Underhill's own terms – backed, it should be said, by wide reading in international affairs, including the history of the Soviet Union and contemporary political thought.[20] A previous article had been similarly ambiguous. In April 1948 he had denounced the Soviet-backed communist coup in Czechoslovakia that had occurred in February, lamenting as he did so the unexplained death of foreign minister Jan Masaryk in March. Here was evidence of communist disregard for basic constitutional procedures that not even the most innocent could ignore, and the way in which "fellow-travelling" members of the Czech Social Democratic party had fallen quickly into line carried lessons for the CCF: "Isn't it about time that the Canadian CCF studied a little more intently what happens to Social Democratic parties in times of crisis if they haven't eliminated their fellow-travellers beforehand?"[21] Not for the first time, this was advice he knew would have a mixed reception. The party had been consistent from the beginning in officially proscribing any association, ideological or organizational, with the Communist Party of Canada (or Labour Progressive Party, as it was known from 1943), but there were many who disagreed with its stance, both inside the party and in the labour movement. Even considering internal divisions, however, his position on foreign policy, fellow-travellers, and Canadian-American relations, and his adoption of "free world" rhetoric, were more in tune with the Liberals than with his own party.

Throughout this period of political assessment and reassessment, a continuing theme of Underhill's writing was the "crisis of liberalism," which he had first started worrying about during the Second World War. One especially striking form it took was his fascination with Arnold Toynbee's massive comparative history of civilizations, A Study of History, which was published in ten volumes over twenty years, from 1934 to 1954, followed by two subsequent volumes of appendices and reflections. If Leo Tolstoy had been the greatest hedgehog of nineteenth-century European literature, Toynbee was his twentieth-century successor, devising a theory of the rise and

fall of civilizations the world over, from Sumerian Meso-
potamia to the present day. He was, as Underhill called him in
the title of his essay reviewing the first six volumes, a "metahistorian" who found the meaning of civilizational change in
a transcendent religious teleology. The reason for Underhill's
interest in a man so different from himself was that Toynbee's
focus on religion as the core of civilization, and his contention
that the West was in decline – if awaiting some possible temporary recovery – typified the "anti-rationalist, anti-scientific,
anti-liberal, anti-democratic" temper of the postwar era and
explained his enormous popularity. He was also capable of
sensible, humane, and insightful analysis when he wrote as a
historian, rather than as a theologian, and even as a theologian
he could be exhilarating and thought-provoking when he
came out from under his pall of pessimism.

Underhill wrote two extended essays on *A Study of History*,
both based on presentations he made at symposia of the
Royal Society of Canada, to which he was elected in 1949.
The first of these carried the title of "Guides and Philosophers
for an Age of Anxiety," a reminder that he was by no means
alone in his absorption in the idea of crisis.[22] Like so many
others – his former student Hilda Neatby in Canada, the
medieval historian Geoffrey Barraclough in England, the
Protestant theologian Reinhold Niebuhr in the United States
– he was beset by the pessimism of his time in the face of
political and social change, domestically and internationally.
This was one reason why he tempered his hopes for the future,
though he also found grounds for optimism. He thought
Toynbee blind to the importance of science, technology, and
political democracy in the modern West, and their potential
for reviving a civilization in apparent decline, though these
matters were admittedly more likely to be noticed by the
"unregenerate secular" historian than the pattern-seeking
prophet of a new age.

Neatby's pessimism was expressed in a stinging attack on
contemporary public school education, *So Little for the Mind*,

in 1953. Commenting on her book in another Royal Society presentation, Underhill agreed with much of what she had to say about the intellectual shortcomings of public schooling, especially at the secondary level, and he came to her defence against the criticisms levelled against her by the "professional educationists." He was disturbed, however, by her underlying almost-theological message, and by her obsession with the philosopher John Dewey, whom she erected into "a kind of personal devil" responsible for all that was wrong with progressive education. Dewey was all the more vulnerable to attack for being among the "baneful American influences" that she and her fellow members of the Royal Commission on National Development in the Arts, Letters, and Sciences – the Massey Commission, named after its chairman, Vincent Massey – had earlier identified as threats to the preservation of a national culture. In actual fact, Dewey had been a "tough-minded" critic on the American left, with an aversion to the sentimental (and ungrammatical) platitudes about "teaching children, not subjects" parroted by his modern descendants. During the 1930s, his disciples had sought to train teachers who would have a "tough, realistic understanding of the social, intellectual, and spiritual crisis" of their time.

If anyone was responsible for the problems of modern education, Underhill thought, it was Egerton Ryerson, the nineteenth-century reformer who had made bureaucratic centralization the norm of Canadian school systems. The real culprit, however, was not a single individual; it was the "anti-intellectual atmosphere of our twentieth-century North American society."[23] Neatby conceded in correspondence with Underhill that she might have been superficial in her treatment of Dewey (if right overall!), but she was unhappy with the labels of "Conservative" and "anti-American." She insisted she was a "Gladstonian Liberal" and no more anti-American than Underhill was anti-British.[24] One doubts that this satisfied his objections. Neatby's religious concerns and her reaction against the inheritance of the Enlightenment placed her in the same camp as Toynbee and were as much an indicator of the modern crisis of liberalism.

Stuart Garson picked up on the ambiguity of Underhill's position on the CCF a second time when he read reports in the *Ottawa Citizen* of a lecture Underhill had delivered at Queen's University in January 1955, as part of the Chancellor Dunning Trust Lecture series. Garson, by this time federal minister of justice in Louis St Laurent's government, posed the same question as he had before. As a devoted listener to Underhill's reviews and commentaries on the CBC, he agreed so often that he wondered if he was becoming a CCFer, but in reading the news account of the lecture, he thought his agreement was really the result of Underhill being a Liberal. Replying promptly this time, Underhill acknowledged with embarrassment his failure to reply to Garson's earlier letter and conceded that maybe he was right: "I'm not any longer a very orthodox C.C.F.er at any rate."[25] In response to Garson's request, he sent him a typescript of the lecture.

He had complained at Queen's of the weakness of the opposition parties in Ottawa, but even more of the success of the Liberals – essentially deriving from the success of Mackenzie King – in occupying the centre of the political spectrum, in the process turning it into the dead centre, for lack of new ideas. The solution, he suggested, lay partly in electoral reform – some system of proportional representation that would make power in Ottawa accord more closely with public opinion – and partly in the creation of party "brain-trusts" that would provide a "mental stimulus" to politics and perhaps lead parties to perform their proper mediating role, educating the public in one direction and politicians in the other. The Liberals, in particular, needed an investment of left-wing ideas to bail them out of intellectual bankruptcy.[26] In asking for a copy, Garson had written that, "as a citizen," he believed that parliamentary democracy worked best in a two-party system with a strong opposition, even if, as a Liberal, he defended his government's record. After reading the talk, he told Underhill that he thought it a "really significant one" to which Liberals ought to pay attention. He had made copies and sent them to all his cabinet colleagues, as well as to "a number of leading civil servants."[27]

Several months later, Underhill retired from the University of Toronto, somewhat against his will, since he had hoped to be appointed chairman of the history department, even if at his age – he had turned sixty-five the previous year – he could only continue at the university on a year-to-year basis. The appointment had gone to his rival Donald Creighton instead, whose chairmanship he did not think he could tolerate. He was offered a soft landing in the form of a position as curator and honorary writer-in-residence of Laurier House in Ottawa, a former residence of both Laurier and Mackenzie King that had become a public museum in 1951 and the repository of King's personal papers. The appointment was made by the Dominion archivist W. Kaye Lamb after consultations with Liberal party insider J.W. Pickersgill, and with Pearson, then minister of external affairs. It seemed especially suitable since it would enable Underhill to work uninterruptedly on his Blake book.[28] Appointment to a job presiding over an institution named after the leading Liberal prime minister of Canada and housing the papers of the man next in line to the title, with the expectation that he would use the opportunity to write his long-awaited biography of the greatest Liberal leader who had not attained the office, did nothing to quiet speculation about Underhill's true political colours.

Whatever shade of pink or red these might be, he was in his element at Laurier House. He operated a kind of daytime salon, as old and new friends dropped by to visit. A close colleague was R. MacGregor Dawson, a senior political scientist whom Underhill had known since the 1930s, when Dawson

had asked him to read the manuscript of a volume of documents on imperial relations that he was preparing. Underhill
had obliged with numerous suggestions about documents to
be included, as well as about Dawson's introduction. "It is
really stimulating to get a broadside such as yours," Dawson
had responded in warm appreciation.[29] At the time a professor at the University of Saskatchewan, he had moved on to
Toronto, as Underhill had, in 1937. Now he was at Laurier
House working on the first volume of the official biography
of Mackenzie King, giving Underhill an opportunity to talk
about one of his favourite subjects. The curatorship aside, he
also made contact with people at Carleton University, which
led to a close affiliation over the next decade and a half, and
to his helping to organize a local branch of the Canadian
Political Science Association.[30]

If his connections were increasingly Liberal and his lectures
and writings at least open to Liberal interpretation, an equally
striking indication of his fluid state of mind was the changing
temper of his discourse. He was less angry, less impatient, and
less aggressively disputatious in what he wrote. His flippancy
became more good-natured, his mockery more gentle, including of himself. Elected president of the Royal Society in 1958,
he began his inaugural address disarmingly: "These are the
reflections of an elderly displaced person out of the nineteenth
century, a homeless liberal." What followed, though, was no
lament for a bygone era, but an acute analysis of the recovery
of conservatism since the end of the Second World War and
the accompanying revival of religious belief – citing the
American literary scholar Daniel Aaron's remark that "Dostoevsky now carries more weight with undergraduates than
Karl Marx" – and what both trends meant for the future of
liberalism. Listing the half-dozen "leading conservative writers" advertised as contributing to a recent issue of the new
American conservative journal *National Review*, and noting
that all but one had been Marxists in the 1920s and 1930s,
he suggested that the intellectual weakness of Canadian

conservatism might be explained by the fact that "not enough of our intellectuals went Marxian in the 1930's, and so they aren't around now to repent in the 1950's."[31] He was no less capable of barbed observation, that is, nor any less critically minded, but the perspective was that of a man drily bemused by the twists and turns of history, and perhaps by the realization that the achievements of the political and intellectual struggles of his lifetime were impermanent.

An "outburst of first-class conservative writing" in the United States, he went on, had produced books by Clinton Rossiter, Russell Kirk, and Peter Viereck, as well as essays in journals like the new *National Review*. He appreciated its quality, as he had appreciated Walter Lippmann thirty years before, Thomas Hobbes thirty years before that, and Toynbee in the present, but he had no doubt it was part and parcel of a general reaction against liberal and democratic beliefs, even if the backroom advisors of the Republican administration in Washington or the recently elected Conservative government in Ottawa were unlikely to have read any of it. In practice, the revival of conservatism signalled the leadership of businessmen, not conservative intellectuals. A similar reaction was also evident in "liberal revisionist" interpretations of American history and society, by writers as diverse as J.K. Galbraith, Reinhold Niebuhr ("the most penetrating and illuminating writer on politics whom I read"), Arthur Schlesinger Jr, and Richard Hofstadter, all of whom expressed a disillusionment and pessimism that contrasted with the confident and optimistic faith in progress of the years before the Second World War.

As usual, Canadians would be affected by the shifting winds from the south, even while denying their impact. The nationalist report of Walter Gordon's Royal Commission on Canada's Economic Prospects was more Conservative than Liberal; Neatby's indictment of public education was much like that offered by the American historian Arthur Bestor in *Educational Wastelands: The Retreat from Learning in Our Public Schools* (1953); and Canadian historian J.M.S. Careless's essay stressing the importance of "metropolitan business" in the making of Canada was an example of northern liberal revisionism. Other straws in the wind were John Farthing's paean to monarchy, *Freedom Wears a Crown* (1957), though Underhill thought it so blind to the realities of Canadian history as to carry little authority, and Donald Creighton's sympathetic biography of John A. Macdonald. Creighton had also delivered a tirade against "the Liberal Interpretation of Canadian history" in his presidential address to the CHA in 1957, in which his former Toronto colleague was an unnamed but clearly leading offender. "On the whole," Underhill remarked, "Professor Creighton's anti-liberalism and anti-Americanism strike me as being too apoplectic to give much intellectual assistance to the smooth public-relations team who are introducing the new Conservatism in the form of practical politics at Ottawa." Moral seriousness, for Underhill, did not preclude irony. For all the signs of a coming dark age, he felt sure that in the brave new conservative world that was coming into being, "when everybody has been successfully adjusted socially," some young student, in some university library, would stumble across the writings of Mill, Bertrand Russell, Charles Beard, or C. Wright Mills. "At that moment," he concluded, "a liberal political movement will start all over again."[32]

The CCF itself moderated its basic platform in 1956, replacing the Regina Manifesto with the Winnipeg Declaration of Principles. Underhill welcomed the change, especially the removal of the rallying cry at the end of the Manifesto: "No C.C.F. Government will rest content until it has eradicated capitalism and put into operation the full programme of socialized planning which will lead to the establishment in Canada of the Cooperative Commonwealth." This had probably been "too emphatic" even in 1933, he wrote in a commentary published in the Toronto *Globe and Mail*, but he reminded his readers that the free-wheeling capitalism of the time had been "irresponsible in its social attitude," heedless of the impact of widespread unemployment, and without any means of dealing with it. Twenty years later, this had changed. Capitalism was now constrained by state regulations and stronger trade unions, and capitalist orthodoxies had been demolished by the theories of the English economist John Maynard Keynes. There was now a mixed economy, and it was time – past time, he thought – for Canadian socialism also to modify itself, as British socialism already had done. Its moral ends remained the same; only the means had changed. The surprising thing was, however, that the new platform had received so much press coverage. He thought this could only mean that newspaper editors were not so sure of the permanency of the CCF's minor party status as they otherwise professed. They were right to be nervous of its potential. In Canada there had been only one major party since the 1920s, the Conservatives having never recovered from the disaster of the conscription crisis of 1917. In demonstrating its willingness to change, the CCF had shown that it was still capable of challenging the Conservatives for second-party status, even if it had been a bit slow in going about it.[33]

The Conservatives threw off this calculus by defeating the Liberals in 1957 and forming a minority government, then by winning the biggest electoral landslide in Canadian history in March 1958, including two-thirds of the seats in previously unwinnable Quebec. In his Dunning Trust lecture, Underhill had worried that, in the absence of the political education of the mass electorate that would follow from the creation of party "brain trusts," the ground was fertile for the rise of some "messianic demagogue" in the mould of Social Credit leaders William Aberhart in Alberta or W.A.C. Bennett in British Columbia. An Ontario Aberhart was a particular danger, without some intellectual enlivening of Ontario voters.[34] The election of Conservative leader John Diefenbaker with a massive majority more than fulfilled all his fears. With the CCF reduced to a rump of eight seats, his good wishes to Mike Pearson of only two months earlier must have taken on new meaning. Pearson had replied in a characteristically jovial manner, if nonetheless serious in his undertaking to do his best to follow Underhill's advice: "I couldn't agree with you more," he had written, "about the necessity for the Liberal Party moving in the direction you suggest, especially toward the youth of the country."[35] He had gotten off to a very bad start as leader shortly afterward when he had invited Diefenbaker to simply turn the reins of power back over to the Liberals, which had provided the Conservative leader the opportunity to request a dissolution of Parliament and a new election, to crushing effect. Without the shock of this electoral debacle, however, it is doubtful that Pearson would have had the moral authority to embark on the rebuilding process that followed.

Underhill became involved when he was invited to participate in the Study Conference on National Problems in Kingston in September 1960, what became known afterward as the Kingston Thinkers' Conference, a meeting formally distinct from the party, though endorsed by Pearson (in contrast to King's hostility toward Vincent Massey's earlier conference at Port Hope).[36] It was a step in the policy-making process, however, only insofar as the ideas it generated might be incorporated in the party "rally" that was to come later. Though its influence is not to be exaggerated, the conference was successful in invigorating the party with new blood and new ideas. Among the presentations, the one given by Tom Kent on social security was especially influential. Pearson had appointed Kent his principal secretary, prompted in part by Underhill's letter, and the results were far-ranging. Though Liberals were divided over their support for Keynesian ideas that aimed at stabilizing the economy through social supports and full employment, the people Pearson gathered around him as advisers were all in favour, to the extent that those on the other side objected vehemently. The journalist Bruce Hutchison, long a confidante of Liberal leaders, including Pearson, called it "leftist nonsense": "What is the new Liberalism anyway? Keynes and Kent? Debt and deficit? More government and less taxes? A slight revision of the Regina Manifesto?"[37] In the event, the National Rally of January 1961 strongly endorsed the proposals that came out of Kingston, not least because its policy chair was another left-leaning Pearson adviser, the nationalist Walter Gordon.[38]

The Keynesian bent of the new Liberal policies had been foreshadowed during and after the war by a series of public reports: the *Report on Social Security for Canada* (1943) by Leonard Marsh, who had been a member of the Montreal branch of the LSR; the *White Paper on Employment and Income* (1945), laying out the government's plans for postwar reconstruction; and the "Green Book" proposals that had presented those plans to the Dominion-Provincial Conference on Reconstruction that met in 1945.[39] The ideas were no longer as new, that is, as they had been a quarter-century earlier, even if many in the Liberal party and elsewhere continued to regard them as radical. There were also constitutional and technical limits to the extent to which Keynesian proposals could be put into practice, regardless of the party in power.[40] Nevertheless, the fact that they were no longer dismissed out of hand and gained the traction they did among Liberals was important in shifting the political spectrum toward the left, where it would remain for the next twenty-five years. Liberals were not social democrats, but many of them were open to social democratic ideas.

It soon became apparent that this was enough for Underhill. At Kingston, he did not address a policy session but rather the closing plenary gathering, where he was at pains to declare his independence. He had no particular policy expertise, he said; his speciality was "general invective." He then went on to criticize the Liberal party, Liberal governments, and much of the conference's agenda.[41] However, this was more a sign that he was not prepared to make any commitment of the kind he had made in 1933 than a rejection of the party. That autumn, Macmillan of Canada published a book of his essays, *In Search of Canadian Liberalism*. In a gesture surely carrying more weight than the customary token of an author's regard, he dedicated it to "Mike Pearson."[42]

More explicitly, some months later he reviewed a new book by the CCF stalwart Stanley Knowles on the creation of the New Party – eventually the New Democratic Party – out of an alliance between the CCF and the Canadian Labour Congress. On the basis of the book, Underhill wrote, it was hard to say just what was new about the New Party; "Old Wine in New Bottles" was the title he gave to the review. He criticized Knowles for repeating the standard attacks on the old parties while offering nothing to show that he and his colleagues had asked themselves why their old nostrums had failed to win over voters since they had first been presented in the 1930s. Nor did he show that a party of the left had much to offer in a time when the great problems of economic production that had led to the CCF's birth had actually been solved. Underhill pointed to the example of John F. Kennedy's "New Frontier" in the United States – Kennedy had won the presidency in 1960 – and the emergence of what Arthur Schlesinger called "qualitative liberalism," which he thought better adapted to the needs of the present.[43]

This was an idea not far removed from a distinction Tom Kent made between state action in the service of socialism, which enlarged public participation in production, and state action to create what he called a "welfare economy," which concerned itself with consumption and directed public expenditure toward such things as medical insurance, unemployment benefits, urban renewal, public housing, and education.[44] Underhill put forward the examples of the CBC and the recently created Canada Council in his review of Knowles. He called them instances of "cultural socialism" and suggested they were the result of action by middle-class intellectuals and professionals tied to no one particular party. Class was no longer a basis for party action, he wrote, and it was no longer clear that the "British political framework" contained the lessons for Canada it once had. Instead, Canadians ought to consider the successes of the Democratic Party in the United States. Perhaps it was time to stop asking why the Americans had no Labour party, and to start asking why Canada had no Democratic party. He returned to the same idea in reviewing a new collection of essays, *Social Purpose for Canada*, aimed at doing for the N D P what *Social Planning for Canada* had done for the C C F. The strongest part of the book, he said, was the first section, precisely because it dealt with questions of the quality of life, rather than the machinery of production. Otherwise, the biggest gap in the book was the absence of any discussion of how a "Left party" planned to act in what the economist John Kenneth Galbraith called an "affluent society," in which the challenges lay not in the generation of wealth but its distribution.[45]

For Underhill, then, the answer to those challenges in Canada, and the closest approximation to the Democratic Party of Roosevelt's New Deal and Kennedy's New Frontier, would come from the Liberals and not the New Democratic Party. In the federal election of June 1962, he voted Liberal for the first time since 1911. The election produced a Conservative minority government, which fell within a year amid internal party disputes. In the election that followed, he voted Liberal again. This time it was the Liberals who formed a minority government, and he wrote Pearson a second time to congratulate him on becoming prime minister. He was forced to admit, he said, that big business seemed to have "more potential liberalism in its make-up at present than has our populist democracy," but he urged Pearson, as he had before, to resist pressures to move his party to the centre. He also assured him of his support, pointing to articles he had written in the *Toronto Star* as proof. Nevertheless, "having lived in a state of slightly tempestuous wedded love with the C.C.F. for some twenty-five years, and having broken up that connection on the grounds of incompatibility of temperament," he would not be committing himself to political matrimony again. Pearson replied, also as he had before, by promising to keep the party "where it should be – to the left of the centre."[46]

Elder Statesman

> What makes the political history of any people fascinating,
> exciting, inspiring, is this constant interplay, this ever changing
> tension between ideas and material interests, ideas and power.
> F.H. Underhill, "Canadian Intellectuals and Politics," 1967

Despite being slowed down by advancing age and ill health, Underhill maintained a pace of writing, teaching, and public speaking in the 1960s that might have been the envy of younger men. Now in his seventies, he suffered a series of strokes after moving to Ottawa, and his ulcer continued to bother him, but he remained active.[1] He began writing more often for the daily press – the *Toronto Star*, the *Globe and Mail*, and the *Winnipeg Free Press* – and commercial magazines – *Maclean's* and the *Globe and Mail Magazine* – than for the *Canadian Forum* or the *New Republic*. He had written for such outlets before, but supplementary to the intellectual journals. Now the priority was reversed. This undoubtedly was motivated partly by his meagre pension and the need to earn even more income from his writing in retirement than he had previously done, though one suspects that he was also happy to be writing for a wider audience than the small number of intellectually and politically engaged readers that the smaller journals served.[2] The *Globe* paid him $40 a time for book reviews, the *Star* $60 for a bi-weekly column, which rose to $75 when the column became syndicated. The editors at both papers were pleased by the quality and quickness of his contributions.[3] He wrote other pieces for payment as well: the annual entry on Canada for the *Encyclopedia Americana Annual* ($78.50), the entries on Laurier and King for the *Encyclopedia Canadiana* in 1956 ($100), and the entry on Laurier for the *World Book Encyclopedia* in 1963.[4]

He also kept up a wide personal, professional, and political correspondence. He sent out offprints of his publications, as he had always done, and received comments and expressions of appreciation in return. Clinton Rossiter, for example, responded to his Royal Society address on the new conservatism by saying that Underhill had possibly been the only person who had understood just what he had been doing in his book. Sometimes, those who received an offprint sent it on to someone else. Others simply responded to something Underhill had written, or Underhill sent off a comment of his own to a friend or acquaintance.[5] When Harry Crowe was dismissed from United College in Winnipeg in 1958, Underhill wrote to Tom Kent, objecting to the editorial support the *Free Press* was giving to the college, and he encouraged friends in university administrations to do what they could to find a job for Crowe, and for J.H. Stewart Reid and Kenneth McNaught, who had resigned from their college appointments in protest. "Giving advice to university heads is not exactly in my line," he wrote W.A. MacIntosh, principal of Queen's University, but the treatment of Crowe had been "outrageous."[6]

Other colleagues besides MacGregor Dawson benefited from his critical reading, sometimes directly, sometimes via a publisher's report or an assessment for a granting agency, and often in book reviews. He commented at length on Ramsay Cook's revised PhD thesis, on its way to becoming *The Politics of John W. Dafoe and the Free Press* (1963), a subject Underhill knew as well as anyone. He gave it high praise – "one of the most interesting and enlightening studies that I have ever read from a young historian" – while offering many pages of questions and comments. He was especially put out by the tendency of the younger generation to be "a little bit too superior" in their attitude toward their elders who had lived through the events they were studying without having had the benefit of knowing how things would turn out. Hindsight was twenty-twenty.[7] He made the same point rather more sharply in reviewing a book by political scientist James Eayrs on Canadian foreign policy during the 1930s, acknowledging his own errors of judgment but wondering if the observers of the 1960s were any less innocent in their moralistic criticisms of US imperialism.[8] In Cook's case, the criticism was considerably more tempered, and he may well have felt the blast of an Underhill critique to be as invigorating as Dawson had.

Meanwhile, Underhill read as much and as widely as ever. He read the English writer and scientist C.P. Snow's "The Two Cultures and the Scientific Revolution" (1959), the American literary critic Leslie Fiedler's *Love and Death in the American Novel* (1960), the critic George Steiner's *Tolstoy or Dostoevsky: An Essay in the Old Criticism* (1961), and the American philosopher Eric Hoffer's *The True Believer* (1951). He read E.H. Carr's *What Is History?* (1961) – originally the George Macaulay Trevelyan Lectures at Cambridge University – as it came out serially in the BBC *Listener*, having earlier read Carr on international relations and the history of the Soviet Union; he read Bertrand Russell's *Autobiography* (1967–69), as he had earlier read his tracts and writings on philosophy and politics; and he continued to read everything written by Walter Lippmann. He read Richard Hofstadter's *Anti-Intellectualism in American Life* (1963), Seymour Martin Lipset's *The First New Nation* (1963), Louis Hartz's *The Founding of New Societies* (1964), Edmund Wilson's *O Canada: An American's Notes on Canadian Culture* (1965), and Samuel H. Beer's *British Politics in a Collectivist Age* (1967). He read Donald Creighton, Vernon Fowke, D.C. Masters, and J.M.S. Careless on Canadian history. In all cases, and in many others, he made copious notes as he went along. There was no keeping up with Underhill, even in his seventies.[9]

More than anything else, however, it was the politics of the present that continued to engage his interest. He still did not sever his relations with the CCF entirely, contributing money to the election campaigns of Stanley Knowles in Winnipeg North Centre, and joining in efforts to create a retirement fund for M.J. Coldwell after he was defeated in the 1958 election and was forced to step down as leader of the CCF in its last days. Underhill served as honorary treasurer of the fund-raising committee and spoke warmly of his old friend and colleague at a luncheon held in his honour in January 1962. Opening his talk, he alluded obliquely to his own change of allegiance, and perhaps to the internal tensions of the NDP as it shed its CCF skin, in saying that everyone present was there individually and not as the representative of "any particular party affiliation or ideology." "Party politics!" he sighed. They were essential to a free society, but in Canada their intellectual quality had been falling in recent years. Coldwell had distinguished himself over his entire career by seeking to raise "the intellectual and moral" level of politics, and by putting "the general good" ahead of the interests of regions and groups. Individual MPs bore some responsibility for the calibre of debate in the House of Commons, and Coldwell, in taking on more than his share, had been the "greatest private member of Parliament of our day."[10] It was a generous tribute to his former ally in party struggles.

In the nature of things, more and more of his political contacts were with Liberals and the Liberal party. Though his involvement was neither as full nor as intense as it had been with the CCF, he offered advice and sought to stimulate ideas. Shortly after the Kingston conference, he corresponded with Senator Charles G. "Chubby" Power, a sometime Mackenzie King cabinet minister, about "socialistic liberalism" and recommended he read the last volume of Arthur Schlesinger Jr's biography of Franklin Roosevelt, which had just come out. A year later, John Turner, a young Montreal lawyer who had been recruited by Pearson to run as a Liberal candidate for

Parliament, invited him to speak at a Study Conference on Canadian Issues – a kind of mini-Kingston – organized by English-speaking party members in Montreal.[11] In 1967, he spoke at the convention of the Canadian University Liberal Federation, and afterward Jean-Luc Pepin, at the time minister of energy, mines, and resources in Pearson's cabinet, asked him for a copy of his talk, borrowing a page from Stuart Garson. On another occasion, Underhill lectured Liberals on what they might learn from the CCF, pointing out Woodsworth's role in bringing intellectuals into politics and calling it "one of the great innovations of the CCF."[12]

At the same time, he began receiving numerous honours in recognition of the national stature that he had achieved. He was awarded honorary degrees from six universities (Queen's, Carleton, Toronto, Saskatchewan, Manitoba, and York), the Tyrrell Medal of the Royal Society of Canada for "outstanding work in the history of Canada," and the Canada Council Medal for achievement in the "arts, humanities, or social sciences."[13] In 1960, his collection of essays, *In Search of Canadian Liberalism*, received the Governor General's Literary Award for Non-fiction. If social democracy had entered the mainstream, so had Underhill. He was becoming a senior statesman in the intellectual and political wars of his time and the Grand Old Man of Canadian liberalism, much as William Ewart Gladstone had become the Grand Old Man of English liberalism in the late nineteenth century.

Two books helped to confirm and expand his reputation. The first was his award-winning collection of essays. Proposed in 1955 by John Gray, president of the Macmillan Company of Canada, the book had a rocky road to publication. Kildare Dobbs, Macmillan's senior editor, rejected Underhill's first version (with Gray's agreement) on the grounds that it was "too long and too diffuse." He suggested that it might be cut in half. His candidates for deletion included the essays on Woodsworth ("a disappointment"), J.W. Dafoe ("Somewhat sketchy?"), J.S. Ewart ("Rather heavy going?"), Toynbee and Carr ("Relevance not obvious"), Upper Canadian radicalism ("Too special?"), and the party system in Canada ("Dated?"). Many of the suggestions must have seemed baffling to Underhill, in view of what he had spent most of his life writing about. He came back with a reduced version, but this too was deemed too long, now because of rising publication costs.[14] Disheartened, and hampered by illness, he needed prodding to bring the project to completion. Opting for editorial excisions of some of the essays, he finally submitted a revised manuscript in November 1958, which, after further revisions, was ready for publication a year later.[15] Costs were subsidized by the Social Science Research Council of Canada. Ewart, Toynbee, and Carr were gone; the others remained.

Along the way, Dobbs asked if he might consider including an autobiographical introduction (deleting another piece to make room). As a result, Underhill produced the first of several autobiographical essays he was to write over the following decade. Quietly engaging, as was so much of what he wrote in this period, it touched lightly on some of the high points of his public life – his academic appointments at the University of Saskatchewan and Toronto, his involvement with the *Forum*, the LSR, and the CCF, the influence of Dafoe and Woodsworth – and on some of its themes, as they appeared to him in retrospect. Born a "North York Presbyterian Grit" – by now a virtual badge of personal identity – he had never been destined to "belong to the Establishment," a characteristic, he wrote in mild self-deprecation, that had seemed in his younger days to be "one of my particular virtues." Others called him a "natural minoritarian." He had always found, in any case, his "most congenial companions among those who were protesting against something or other." Since first voting Liberal in 1911, he had opted for minority parties somewhat to its left (but not too far) and expected to continue doing so for the rest of his life (this was written in 1959). He also noted some of his second thoughts – for example, about the "far-reaching socialism of the Regina Manifesto" – and how his efforts to act on them had made him realize he was not cut out to be a politician. He was now less interested in the fortunes of political parties than in the "climate of opinion" that governed their actions.[16] Any reader who knew his work would have known this was less a new interest than another shift in his priorities.

The book was widely praised on publication. The journalist Don McGillvray picked up on Underhill's self-described outsider status, describing him as "not a stormy petrel of politics, but a kind of lonely political seagull, flying between the Socialist sea and the Liberal shore, perching now on a floating spar, now on a rock, but finding no permanent resting place." Robert Fulford called the collection "an almost perfect political book ... passionate and sophisticated, learned and lively." The reviews in academic journals were equally glowing. Noting how much Underhill had enjoyed himself throughout his life, "trying to save politics from the politicians," the McGill political scientist J.R. Mallory thought that he stood up pretty well "in backward view": his liberalism "was of the tough and sober kind that never had illusions about the perfectability [sic] of mankind." Mallory recommended the essays to the "self-confident" young men and women then trying to renovate both the Liberal party and the C C F. Writing in the *American Historical Review*, Mason Wade of the University of Rochester introduced Underhill to an American audience, calling the book "provocative, stimulating, and beautifully written."[17] The Governor General's Award must have seemed to Underhill like icing on the cake.

The second book that gained him wide attention was *The Image of Confederation*, the published version of his C B C Massey Lectures of 1963. The annual series had begun two years earlier, making Underhill's the third, after the inaugural lecturer Barbara Ward, a British economist and a leading commentator on third world development and underdevelopment, and the literary critic (and Underhill's close friend) Northrop Frye. The C B C's Bernard Trotter extended the invitation in a letter of 18 January 1963, and Underhill replied on 20 January with a proposed outline of his lectures.[18] Not only newspaper editors were impressed by his promptness and speed. The lectures themselves offered listeners and readers a kind of Essential Underhill. In the decade of Canada's centenary he decided to discuss, not so much what had happened in the previous one hundred years, as how Canadians had viewed their country and its nationhood over that time. The result was a series of short essays – short enough to be orally delivered in the half-hour period then allotted to the lectures on C B C radio – on the changing climate of Canadian opinion, amounting to an intellectual history of the new nationality launched in 1867.

His style and his ideas were both on full display. The absence of colonial Jeffersons, Madisons, and Hamiltons to guide their people at the time of the country's founding left an abiding weakness in its national life, while one of its founding myths was that union had been necessary to defend against an expansionist US: "Somewhere on Parliament Hill in Ottawa," he said early in his opening lecture, "during our centenary celebrations in 1967, there should be erected a monument to this American ogre who has so often performed the function of saving us from drift and indecision."[19] Repeatedly directing his listeners' attention to the implications of past actions for present conditions, he spent much of that first lecture on the differing understandings of the meaning of Confederation for English- and French-speaking Canadians. When immediately the country looked westward to Rupert's Land for new agricultural opportunities – again to forestall American expansion, though also driven by George Brown's Ontario nationalism – Manitoba was established as a bilingual province (first round to Quebec), only to be overwhelmed by English-speaking settlers (second round to Ontario) and dominated by business enterprises under English-Canadian and American management: "Hence our present discontents."[20]

Those discontents, manifested in the Quiet Revolution in Quebec and the emergence of the Front de libération du Québec, meant that "the national question" figured more prominently in Underhill's thinking about Canada than it had in the past. His theme for the lectures as a whole was the proposition, originally put forward by the French philosopher Ernest Renan, that a nation was not defined by ethnicity and religion, but was rather "a body of people who have done great things together in the past and who hope to do great things together in the future."[21] Capacious as this definition seemed, the challenges of nationhood were nevertheless substantial and its peaceful achievement full of risks, as Underhill went on to show. Nationalism, liberal and idealistic in its beginnings, as seen in the innocent hopes of the Canada First movement, turned before long into the hard practicalities of Macdonald's National Policy and a railway to the Pacific, and contained within itself "some sinister totalitarian potentialities" that only became evident in the twentieth century.

He devoted an entire lecture to "French-English Relations in Canada," in which he affirmed that Laurier was "the greatest of all Canadians" – it was his opening sentence – and that the "composite bi-racial, bi-cultural party, uniting both French and English voters, [was] one of our great political inventions." Elsewhere, his discussion of imperial relations was framed by Laurier's decision to send troops to fight in the Boer War (1899–1902) and the protest this evoked from the Quebec nationalist (and then Liberal MP) Henri Bourassa. Laurier's response had been that failure to do so would result in a deep national divide. The decision, and the divide – new reason for bitterness in the "long, unending, domestic cold war between Ontario and Quebec" – marked a watershed in Canada's relations with Britain, Underhill argued, and set the agenda of debate for the next half-century.[22] He had been coming to these conclusions over a long period of time, but the central role they played in what was effectively a synthesis of his thought at the time showed once more how the questions he asked of the past responded to social, political, and intellectual change in the present.

Many of his older concerns were also evident: in his characterization of Macdonald's politics as "government of the people, by lawyers, for big business" and its consequences in a Darwinian economic system in which "the lion's share continues to be distributed to the lions"; in his remembrance of the promise of reform after World War I and especially of Woodsworth's ideal – quoting the words of W.L. Morton's recently published *The Kingdom of Canada* (1963) – of a "politics of collective concern for the welfare of the individual in a society collectively organized"; and in his warning to Quebec intellectuals that society was not governed by philosopher-kings but by "hard-boiled, practical administrators," whether they were socialist or not. The overriding concern of his lectures, however, was that Canadians had yet to achieve "any clear, distinctive image of Canada" in their minds and were approaching the second century of their country's existence with little confidence in its future.[23] In saying so, he was striking what would be the dominant note of the sixties, and together with Morton's *The Canadian Identity* (1961), George Grant's *Lament for a Nation: The Defeat of Canadian Nationalism* (1965), and Ramsay Cook's *Canada and the French-Canadian Question* (1966), *The Image of Confederation* would be among the landmark texts of the decade in English-speaking Canada. When the last of these came out, Robert Fulford wrote in the *Toronto Star* that historians were "the great social thinkers of Canada, the people who shape our souls and define our aims," citing Underhill, Donald Creighton, and a handful of others, along with Cook, in evidence.[24]

A project Underhill did not complete was his Blake book. As late as 1960, he explained the absence of anything on Blake from his Macmillan essay collection by saying that he hoped "to deal with him in another volume."[25] This was not to be. Many at the time and since have regarded this as a professional failure. A.R.M. Lower had earlier said as much in congratulating Underhill on his review of Bruce Hutchison's 1953 biography of Mackenzie King, *The Incredible Canadian*, in the *Forum*; however, Lower had continued, he should resist the *Forum* and get on with his Blake book: "One's energies should go into permanent writing."[26] In the citation for Underhill's Tyrrell Medal, J.M.S. Careless wrote that the award was less in recognition of his writing of Canadian history than his teaching of it and his stimulation of ideas, and Mason Wade, in reviewing Underhill's collection of essays, concluded that their quality made one yearn for "the books that were never written" because the demands of students and "the present hour" came first.[27] Even the editor of the Festschrift organized in his honour wrote that he was "not really a historian, but a student of ideas and political institutions and a commentator on politics," while Carl Berger, in his history of English-Canadian historical writing, later described him as "really a political journalist." Though his ideas "raised profoundly significant questions about history," Berger concluded, he was more a "negative critic" than "a constructive thinker or a creative writer of large-scale projects." Plagued by doubts himself, Underhill thought in the end that his involvement in current affairs had taught him more about politics, past and present, than it had cost him in scholarly production.[28] In this he was undoubtedly correct.

It was true that his absorption in current affairs got in the way of his Blake project, as he had complained to Frank Scott in 1941 and to others since, but that was not the reason he did not finish. The project defeated him. Possibly, in making his way through Blake's political machinations, his resignations and attempted resignations, his inconsistencies, and even his sometimes interminable speeches, he concluded in the end that Blake was not the great intellectual he had originally thought him to be.[29] His own conception of politics, in any case, came to rest less on the need for principled leadership and more on a belief that principle had to be combined with conciliation. Yet, even if his enthusiasm for his subject lessened over time, resumption of his research and writing was ostensibly his purpose in taking up his appointment at Laurier House in 1955, and he still insisted on describing Blake as an intellectual in a lecture he gave at Carleton University the following year.[30]

The fact was that the historical monograph was not his natural mode of expression. Nor was immersion in the past, in such a way that he relived it for himself and communicated what it was like for his readers (a prerequisite of effective biography), ideally suited to his temperament. He was much better at making or developing a point in an essayistic manner. This is nowhere more apparent than in his unfinished draft chapters of the biography, which read as though he had taken on the garb of a rather old-fashioned narrative historian, out of a sense of obligation to the genre. It is a tribute to his writing abilities that he could master such a different mode, to the extent that, presented with those chapters, author unidentified, a reader would never guess that they had been written by Underhill. The prose was flowing and descriptive, in places rather arch in its representation of another time and place. For example, in describing the Irish home of Blake's Hume ancestors, he wrote, "A pleasant country house, more in the English style of Queen Anne's reign than most Irish mansions, Humewood stood in the midst of a rolling demesne in a broad valley among the Wicklow mountains forty miles to the south of Dublin. Its long avenues wound across stretches of park and meadow up to the dark grove of lichen-covered trees that flanked the house and sheltered the high-walled gardens in its rear. At the foot of the southerly avenue, about a mile from the house and dominated by the demesne wall, lay the village of Kiltegan with its ancient church and glebe, divorced long since from its original faith, and devoted now, like so many other old Irish churches to the uses of a household chapel for the estate and a mausoleum for its family."[31] His prose versatility aside, however, it seems clear that in searching for a place to begin, he was drawn ever more deeply into Blake's fascinating family background, but he did not know where to stop, going on and on, chapter after chapter.

A second draft got him to his subject more efficiently, but his subject eluded him. Blake, it must be said, was a highly complicated man and his life was full of sharp twists and turns, not just in the progression of his career in Canadian politics, but in his decision of 1892, at the age of fifty-nine, to accept the invitation of the Irish Nationalist party to take up a seat in the British House of Commons. He returned to Canada fifteen years later – having twice turned down offers of appointment to the Canadian Supreme Court – only after suffering a stroke, and died in 1912. To the present day, only one full-length biography of him has been written, and that one not by an academic but an enterprising professional writer, Joseph Schull. All other writing on him, apart from the lengthy entry in the *Dictionary of Canadian Biography*, is about a portion of his life or some aspect of it.[32] Underhill's own numerous articles remain among the starting places for any study of Blake. Accustomed to writing with a message in mind, Underhill must have reached a point where his reason for beginning the project at all became lost to view.

His last published work on Blake – his Carleton lecture – showed him at ease in his natural mode, taking his listeners (and readers) on a slightly meandering survey of Blake's political career in Canada, touching only briefly on his time overseas. There was nothing new in the lecture, suggesting just how little further research he had done since the early forties at this point, but he deftly sketched Blake's background and character – "a painfully reserved and shy individual, with no capacity for playing the demagogue" – and summarized his liberal views of Empire and nationhood, his role in Alexander Mackenzie's government, and his relations with Laurier. For all of his talent and promise, he had been "the most tragic

failure that has yet appeared in our Canadian public life."[33]
The lecture was the first in a series of seven and was followed,
two lectures later, by one on John A. Macdonald by Donald
Creighton, the second volume of whose magisterial biography
of Macdonald had appeared the year before. Creighton nevertheless began with five pages (of fifteen in total) of withering
sarcasm on the dominance of what he called the "authorized
version" – that is, the "Liberal or Grit interpretation" and,
unmistakably, Underhill's interpretation – of Canadian history.
It required, he said, "a good deal of moral courage" to question even a small part of this conventional wisdom.[34] It was a
foretaste of his presidential address to the Canadian Historical
Association in 1957 and there can be no doubt, reading both
talks, that Underhill's take on Canadian political history had
an impact, as far as Creighton was concerned. In judging
Underhill's output, then, we should be wary of prescriptive
hierarchies. Historical writing takes a variety of forms, and the
essay is one of them. Underhill was no less a historian for
adopting it, or for failing to complete his Blake biography.

There was another way in which his practice of history was
at odds with the practice of modern professional historians:
he was not a historicist. That is, he did not believe that, to
know something, is to know how it evolved over time and
how it came to be what it is in the present. This is an idea that
has its roots in the nineteenth century and remains central to
the justification of history as a discipline, for all the various
methods of historical study that have contended over the past
century. He was not interested in the past in and for itself, or
as a means of understanding the origins of the present; he was
interested in the past for the lessons it could offer, and for
models of thought and action that might be followed in the
present. Like his classics professors at Oxford, he always
related the documents and texts he was reading to the political issues of his own day. He was interested in the past,
in other words, as a guide to the future. That was why he
found the Clear Grits so interesting – not because they *were*

interesting, but because they so clearly anticipated the Pro-gressives; and why he was so interested in men like Blake, George Brown, and Goldwin Smith. This does not this mean, either, that he was not a historian, only that his history was of another kind, what in the eighteenth century would have been called philosophy teaching by example.

He continued writing and speaking throughout the sixties, recapping and summing up the themes of a life in writing. He added his voice to those of others who sought to establish a series of reprints of out-of-print classics of Canadian history and politics – he called them "egg-head paper-backs" – and helped in the establishment of the Carleton Library Series, editing and introducing one of his particular suggestions, André Siegfried's *The Race Question in Canada*.[35] Siegfried, Underhill began his introduction, was "the Tocqueville of Canada," only Canadians had shown so "little taste for that realistic and critical self-knowledge which is the mark of maturity" that he was unknown in the country he had studied so well. In contrast, Tocqueville's *Democracy in America* had become a classic in the United States. Written in 1906, *The Race Question* was remarkably pertinent in the present day, Underhill thought, in its analysis of French-English relations and the Canadian party system. As an anti-clerical French Protestant, Siegfried had viewed religious differences in Canada, and their role in politics, with a modernist detach-ment that was sure to be of interest in the era of the Quiet Revolution in Quebec.[36]

The issue that returned with a vengeance for Underhill was the relations between Canada and the United States. George Grant's *Lament for a Nation* roused his ire as did few other books of that, or any other, decade, though he managed a remarkably balanced assessment of its merits. It was part "cool philosophical treatise" in its treatment of the homoge-nizing force of modern technology, already dealt with by Grant in *Philosophy in the Mass Age* (1959), which Underhill thought "just about the best lecture series that C.B.C. has ever produced"; part "fiery party tract" in its condemnation of the sins of the Liberal party; and part "an expression of family piety" in its nostalgia for the Victorian faith of his grandfathers G.M. Grant and Sir George Parkin. In the party tract, however, Grant showed himself to be "as violently and neurotically anti-American as John Diefenbaker himself," producing passages in the book that seemed to Underhill "emotional drivel." It was not Mackenzie King and his minister of reconstruction C.D. Howe (later minister of trade and commerce under St Laurent) who had brought American influence to Canada, nor even the "capitalist Establishment," but "our democratic masses," who had welcomed the habits and attitudes of "the first mass society in the modern world" with open arms. Finally, Grant argued that conservatism was impossible in the modern era, made irrelevant by the relentless progress of science, which left his readers with little opportunity to get out from under his overwhelming pessimism, except through hints of some kinship with socialism. Liberals, whatever their faults, were more optimistic. Having managed peacefully to free themselves of British rule, liberal Canadians believed in the possibility of a friendly, independent relationship with the United States. They could not guarantee it – they needed to nurture a European "countervailing power" – but they had faith in the future.[37]

Underhill's friend Norman Ward, the University of Saskatchewan political scientist, had questioned his "anti-anti-Americanism" a few years before, not so much because Ward disagreed with it as because he had been inspired as an undergraduate by Underhill's "anti-British" position and it seemed to him that the anti-Americanism of young people in the present was "serving the same liberal ends."[38] Underhill was unpersuaded. Having come to maturity on the edge of the British Empire, he had been caught in the tensions wrought by his attraction to England as a model of intellectual and cultural modernism, even as he had been repelled politically by its imperial and foreign policies; and by his desire to embrace his own country, even as he had been dismayed by its state of continuing colonial dependency. Identification with North America had offered a means of reconciliation, which was only confirmed as the British Empire faded into irrelevance in the decades after World War II. The new anti-Americanism, compound of old toryism and new youthful socialism, was a mystery to him.

A year after his Grant review, he was invited to write the foreword to a book by politically engaged academics who had created a University League for Social Reform in Toronto, emulating the League for Social Reconstruction before them. Underhill noted that "continentalism" had become a "four-letter word" in contemporary parlance and was used as such by many of the book's authors. They seemed unduly satisfied by the idea that Canada's "mosaic" was somehow preferable to the American "melting-pot," and they seemed to think that Canadian international policy was far better suited to the contemporary world than "the 'imperialistic' power politics" of Washington. It was certainly cheaper, he said of the second. In both cases he thought the implied sense of moral superiority toward the US was little different from that of nineteenth-century Canadians, whose attitudes everyone otherwise regarded with condescending "genial irony."[39] It was an issue he could not get away from in the nationalist sixties.

During centennial year, he was invited back to Queen's to give another of the Dunning Trust Lectures, choosing again to return to the subject closest to his heart, intellectuals and politics. Demonstrating his ability, honed over many decades of practice, to win over an audience from the start, he began by alluding to a recent review by Donald Creighton of a biography of Laurier by Joseph Schull (the biographer, later, of Blake), in which Creighton had remarked that Carleton University, whose faculty figured prominently in Schull's prefatory acknowledgments, had taken over the status previously held by Queen's as the intellectual centre of Canadian liberalism. If his listeners detected a note of condescension in his address, Underhill said, they were to understand that its source lay in his role as "visiting staff officer from the intellectual G H Q of Canadian liberals." (It's hard not to think that he got the best of Creighton in their exchanges by virtue simply of his understatement.) He continued in a similarly disarming manner by warning against misleadingly precise social scientific models in identifying intellectuals as a cultural type: "It is sufficient to say at the outset [that] I think that intellectuals generally are people like you and me." As will be apparent by now, Underhill was seldom as innocent as he appeared.

Despite a necessary imprecision, he continued, it was still possible to trace the way the term was actually used and thus to situate its meaning historically. He had found that the word "intellectual" had first been used as a noun in the Dreyfus Affair of turn-of-the-century France. It described people who were willing to be critical of "the establishment," to ask "inconvenient and embarrassing questions about the implications of accepted beliefs or policies," and to ask them "at inconvenient times and in embarrassing ways." They brought ideas to public life, preventing politics from being drowned in "an over-production of ditchwater," citing his old classics professor, Maurice Hutton. There had been too few ideas, and too few intellectuals, in Canadian politics, with dispiriting results: "What makes the political history of any people fascinating, exciting, inspiring, is this constant interplay, this ever changing tension between ideas and material interests, ideas and power." He even retreated from his reconciliation with brokerage politics, saying that those who taught that they were a form of politics "proper" to the US and Canada only performed a "disservice" to their students.

Intellectuals, Underhill argued, were a phenomenon of the twentieth century. At other times individuals very like them had acted differently. From 1867 to 1918, "intellectuals" such as W.A. Foster of Canada First, Edward Blake, Stephen Leacock, and Andrew Macphail, the McGill professor of medicine and editor of *University Magazine*, had acted "merely as

a clerisy" – a term, he noted, invented by Samuel Taylor Cole-
ridge in the early nineteenth century – "expounding the meaning of our communal experience as they saw it." After the
First World War there was a perceptible "change of temper,"
evident in the differences in tone and substance between
University Magazine and the *Canadian Forum*. Intellectuals
became critics, especially on the left, Mackenzie King (if only
briefly) and Woodsworth among them, both "discerning cor-
rectly" that politics in the future would concern "the social
welfare economic planning state." Now it seemed that intellectuals were everywhere, yet Underhill found himself still
dissatisfied, since they seemed to have had little effect on the
level of national debate. Referring his listeners to books by
Lewis Coser and Richard Hofstadter, and to an essay by
the American intellectual historian H. Stuart Hughes, "Is the
Intellectual Obsolete?," he drew their attention particularly to
Hughes's distinction between "genuine intellectuals" and
"mental technicians." The latter were specialists and experts,
while the former were generalists whose thought and action
ranged far beyond their particular field of expertise. Just who
were intellectuals thus varied depending on context, circumstances, and their conception of themselves. Underhill's own
use of the term illustrated its variability, though no one in his
audience at Queen's can have thought by the end of his talk
that he seriously meant to include all of them in his definition
of "the intellectual."[40]

Underhill's Queen's lecture was as close as he ever came to a
statement of his personal credo. His autobiography was
something else. He never did take up a suggestion of John
Gray's that he write his memoirs, but he gave an extended
address of personal reminiscence at a celebration of his eightieth birthday on 26 November 1969.[41] Originally planned for
Carleton, it was moved to the Rideau Club to accommodate

a growing invitation list. The new venue, whether purposely or not, reflected his new status, now welcomed into the Establishment he had needled and resisted for so long. Among the guests were former prime minister Lester Pearson, former finance minister Walter Gordon, former clerk of the Privy Council Robert Bryce, and the president of Carleton and former co-chair of the Royal Commission on Bilingualism and Biculturalism Davidson Dunton. The others – some 125 in all – included friends and colleagues from the fields of politics, journalism, business, and academia. Geraldine MacKenzie, who had been a student in his first history class at Saskatchewan, in 1914, was present. The head table mainly comprised (at Underhill's request) members of the LSR: Eugene Forsey, King Gordon, Joseph Parkinson, Escott Reid, Frank Scott, Graham Spry, and their wives. Scott was one of four people who introduced the guest of honour. The others were Underhill's former student Hilda Neatby, his younger fellow historian Ramsay Cook, and his old friend Mike Pearson. The evening was organized by another former student and friend, the historian H. Blair Neatby, who was aided by the former Liberal MP (and a colleague at Carleton) Pauline Jewett, and Tim Reid, the son of Escott Reid and Underhill's godson. It was a warm, convivial evening, the atmosphere perhaps too cozy by half to an outside critic, but ideally suited to the occasion.[42]

Underhill called his speech his *Apologia pro Vita Sua,* or "The Education of Frank Underhill," cautioning his audience that he had seen a recent review of a memoir by J.K. Galbraith about his years as American ambassador to India, in which the reviewer had complained that, after some 800 pages, "the irony and sarcasm fail, and the self-deprecating wit no longer disguises the boundless vanity." Try as he might, Underhill said, he would no doubt be unable to conceal his own boundless vanity. His was a liberal generation, he began, for whom it was impossible to imagine that radicals of the left might join with radicals of the right – as in the present day – "to liquidate what they call the liberal establishment." He recalled the golden years of pre-World War I Canada and England, recounting stories from his childhood in Stouffville and his student days at Toronto and Oxford. He had especially fond memories of W.S. Milner at Toronto, who had once commended him on a "penetrating remark" he had made about Aristotle's *Politics*. Milner's further discussion showed that the remark had not really been all that penetrating, but, said Underhill, "I still squirm with delight whenever I recall it." He talked about Malcolm Wallace and his introduction to Hobbes – "I have never been the same man since" – and Mill, about G.M. Wrong and his gratitude for Wrong's guidance, and about managing to talk his way into admission to the stacks of the library, then closed to students.

He spent just as much time remembering Balliol College, especially the intellectual excitement it offered, not just in his study of the classics and modern history, but in his engagement with the politics of the time, through clubs, speeches, debates, journals, and the wider culture of pre-war England, especially the novels of H.G. Wells and the plays of G.B. Shaw. Recently rereading some of his favourite books, he had discovered that he had lost his copy of L.T. Hobhouse's *The Metaphysical Theory of the State: A Criticism* (1918), based on lectures the famous New Liberal had given toward the end of the war. Searching in the Carleton library, he found that its copy had belonged to Mike Pearson: "This restored my confidence in Pearsonian liberalism," he gently remarked. He went on to discuss his service in the war and the problem of being "a natural loner" in a military regiment, the lessons of which he had to relearn all over again when he later became involved in the socialist movement. His return to the west in the twenties, his admiration for Dafoe and Woodsworth, his absorption in prairie politics, his return to Toronto, and his involvement in the LSR and the CCF: all of this he described with a light touch and an occasionally acerbic comment. It is testimony to the respect in which he was held, and to the interest of his remembrances, that his audience gave him their close attention for over two hours.

He concluded on an elegiac note. The LSR's success had been limited. It probably had much less to do with whatever success the CCF had achieved than its now-superannuated members would like to think. More important had been the CCF leadership, in Woodsworth and Coldwell, whom he was proud to have followed. The Canadian party system had not been remodelled along British lines as they – the members of the LSR – had hoped, and the intellectual level of politics had not noticeably risen, to judge from the present. Their biggest weakness had been never to have made a case that proved attractive to French Canada, which probably resulted from a wider failure among English Canadian academics and intellectuals, outside of McGill and including himself, to have studied it seriously. Their biggest mistake had been to expect "too much of politics." A society could produce a great culture without a great politics, but it could not produce a great politics except on the foundation of a great culture. In the 1930s, Canada's had been a colonial culture. He felt rather sad, he confessed, that he had never produced the intellectual history of Canada for which he had been, "as a matter of fact, rather well prepared." Doubts lingered about the choices he had made.

The birthday party was well covered in the press, partly because of the journalists in the crowd. Peter C. Newman, who had been one of the guests, called it a moving tribute to "the most influential thinker this country has so far produced," though he also noted that it seemed at times like "a self-congratulatory farewell for a political generation."[43] Ramsay Cook reported on the event in the column he wrote in *Le Devoir*. Noting the irony of a dinner held in the Rideau Club to celebrate the birthday of one of the leading radicals of English-speaking Canada, he paid tribute to Underhill's passionate pursuit of his own way and his fearless criticism of conventional politics. He recounted for his readers the history of Underhill's role in the CCF and the LSR, picking up on his concluding remarks about their failure to attract support in Quebec. For all of the differences between English- and French-Canadian nationalists, Cook ventured to suggest that they shared some things in common; in the cases of Underhill and his near contemporary, the nationalist historian and intellectual Abbé Lionel Groulx, they were very different in many ways, but they shared a belief that politics was too important to be left to the politicians, and that the moral and intellectual tone of Canadian public life was in serious need of revitalizing.[44]

Tributes to Underhill continued to come in. In the spring of 1970, the *Forum* published a special issue to mark its fiftieth anniversary, in which his early role figured prominently. In his own contribution, he quoted a long passage from a novel by H.G. Wells which, he said, he had been fond of quoting in the 1930s. The main character of the novel, *The Autocracy of Mr. Parham*, was an Oxford don who aspired to the editorship of one of those highbrow weeklies that gave "intellectual guidance" to its readers on the ways of the world. Such a fine journal it would be: "It was to be understanding, advisory, but always a little aloof. It was to be bold at times, stern at times, outspoken at times, but never shouting, never vulgar. As an editor one partakes of the nature of God ... and without God's responsibility for the defects and errors of the universe you survey."[45] Underhill was more likely to play the court jester than the priest or the biblical prophet at this time of his life. A month or so later, at the CHA annual meeting in Winnipeg, he joined Arthur Lower in a session that was dedicated as much to recognizing the contribution the two of them had made to Canadian history as to marking the hundredth anniversary of the birth of the province of Manitoba.[46]

Underhill died on 16 September 1971, after suffering another stroke. He was two months shy of his eighty-first birthday. At his funeral, Joe Parkinson delivered a moving eulogy, in which he paid special tribute to the courage Underhill had demonstrated as an intellectual, a quality perhaps easily forgotten when there was so much else to attract one's attention. Parkinson wanted to select the "vital elements" of Underhill's character, he said: "Perhaps the first of these is his great moral courage, his willingness to stand alone, if need be, in proclaiming the truth as he saw it. And his willingness to accept the public hostility and punishment that his views might entail. As we all know, there were circumstances in the thirties and forties when his courage was severely tested."[47] Parkinson's testament said almost as much about the affection and respect that members of the L S R had for one another, transcending the many disagreements among them, as it did about Underhill. H. Blair Neatby wrote the obituary notice in the *Canadian Historical Review*, the leading journal of the historical profession in Canada. Underhill's "scholarship and his involvement in the present," he wrote, "marked everything he wrote, whether it was for a newspaper or a learned journal."[48] It was a simple thing to say, but it covered a lot of ground.

Epilogue

The disposition to disagree, to reject and to dissent – however irritating it may be when taken to extremes – is the very lifeblood of an open society.

Tony Judt, *Ill Fares the Land*, 2010

The premise of Underhill's conception of a climate of opinion was that the values and assumptions of different "climates" were more or less foreign to one another, the foreignness increasing with the passage of time. Those distant chronologically required a greater effort of the historical imagination to understand, when understanding was possible at all, than those in closer proximity, though even those that seem superficially familiar may be stranger than we think. The job of the historian was to set them in relation to each other and try to discover their connections, as well as to show how they shaped the public debates of their day. Underhill had derived the idea, at least in part, from Carl Becker's *The Heavenly City of the Eighteenth-Century Philosophers*, "that unique paragon of all modern works of historical criticism," though Becker also believed that tracing the influence of any one writer on another was a futile endeavour.[1] The important thing to notice was that the writer influenced was predisposed, or at least receptive, to the ideas thought to have been transmitted from one to the other; that is, he was immersed in a climate of opinion in which those ideas made sense.[2] Anyone today, then, who seeks to comprehend the intellectual context

of even half a century ago finds that the attitudes and assumptions of that time lie behind a barely visible screen.

Most obviously, the left liberal, social democratic ideas that
emerged before the First World War and entered the mainstream of Anglo-American thought after the Second were displaced at the end of the twentieth century – displaced in the
mainstream – by the descendants of the new conservatism
whose rise Underhill traced in the 1950s, and whose impact he
feared threatened his own intellectual dispositions. His fear
was well founded. Nineteenth-century localist, anti-statist radical liberalism had undergone a mutation in the early twentieth century into a belief that central government, properly
informed, could act in the interests of the general good – indeed,
was necessary to the advancement of the general good – while
the conservatism of Underhill's time underwent its own mutation into the decentralist neo-conservatism of the present day,
hostile to state activism of almost any kind. One element of
continuity from the first liberalism to the second was a belief in
the primacy of politics. Whether or not Underhill was right
in judging the LSR's high expectations of politics to have been a
mistake, he was certainly right in identifying politics as central
to the aspirations and actions of himself and his colleagues, just
as it had been central to those earlier radicals who had believed
that the extension of the franchise, and the participation in
politics that would follow, would educate voters, in and of
itself, and make them active citizens in the political community.
By contrast, Marxists on the social democrats' left and conservatives on their right both believed, in very different ways, that
the economy and production came first. Today, disenchantment with politics is widespread, in part as a result of the con-
certed anti-politics of the new right, while political discourse is
dominated by the needs of the economy. Marxism having lost
its political force, those needs are framed entirely in the language of business. Underhill may be turning over in his grave.

If he was correct in foreseeing the resurgence of conservatism, he did not see that it would take a form quite different

from that which confronted liberals and social democrats in the third quarter of the twentieth century. Perhaps he ought to have paid more attention to Diefenbaker populism at home than to the philosophic conservatism discussed by Clinton Rossiter in the United States. The conservatism that came to dominate politics had little interest in conserving very much of anything, except in gestures toward royalty and the military past, in the case of Canada; it was, instead, a radical movement, a counter-revolution, led in the Anglo-American democracies by Margaret Thatcher in Great Britain, taken up by Ronald Reagan in the United States, and given legitimacy by the fall of the Berlin Wall and the collapse of the Soviet Union.[3] It was brought to Canada somewhat belatedly – in this, at least, Underhill would not have been surprised – by Preston Manning's Reform Party and put into practice by Stephen Harper's reconstructed Conservatives, though its arrival was also facilitated by corporate Liberals who, under the prime ministership of Jean Chrétien, turned against their own history and closed the door that Lester Pearson had opened to the left. If Underhill's role as an intellectual paved the way for younger like-minded critics after him, such as Ramsay Cook, it also did so for more recent critics on the right, such as the political scientist Tom Flanagan. Liberals and New Democrats have been confused and uncertain about how best to respond to a conservative politics of conviction, ideology having historically manifested itself on the left wings of their own parties and movements.

Accompanying this displacement of social democracy have been cultural changes that have also altered the mainstream. The place occupied by intellectuals has been diffused in more recent times, as culture itself has become decentred, in the language of postmodernism. The grand master narratives in which one might locate one's society and its stage of development have dissolved, as has the idea of moral authority that enabled intellectuals like Underhill to think of their role as in some way educational, disseminating ideas and showing the way forward, if only by exposing the self-interest of those in power and demonstrating that there actually were alternatives when those in power said there were none. Intellectuals today are everywhere – in this also Underhill glimpsed the future – but they hold no special position. The "little magazines" that gave them a platform – those that were political rather than literary in their orientation – have lost their special place on the newsstand, if they still exist (the *Forum* does not), and no one any longer thinks there is such a thing as a singular public. Instead, there are many publics, and the means of reaching them are beyond counting in the digital age. Even within a single medium, such as the daily newspaper, intellectuals find themselves on the op-ed page (in its print or online version) side by side with other commentators and observers, from think-tank experts and management consultants to politicians (active and retired) and professional political strategists, and from religious writers to satirists and humorists. They are no longer uniquely critical in their posture, or even necessarily critical at all, sometimes turning into men- or women-of-letters in the manner of the nineteenth century European *fin-de-siècle*.[4] They function differently from Underhill simply by virtue of their ubiquity.

Implicit in the idea of "leading the way forward" was the assumption that there was a way to the future, and that the future promised improvement if the right way was chosen. Appearances to the contrary notwithstanding, Underhill was an optimist and an idealist, though no utopian. His cynicism was all on the surface, a play of wit and rhetoric. Not far below that surface was a faith in progress, tempered by realism, another link of continuity with his radical liberal ancestors. That underlying faith made those who turned their backs on progress – fascists, totalitarian statists, religious revivalists (and fundamentalists), conservative resurrectionists – all the more frustrating and all the more threatening, and the need to react defensively in response to them all the more necessary. Still, dismaying as the course of the twentieth century undoubtedly seemed, he did not join Arnold Toynbee in his mood of doom and gloom. He persisted in his belief in progress, though he limited his expectations to the achievement of progress by increments. Here, too, however, there has been change since Underhill's day. No one any longer believes in progress; at least, no one would say that a belief in progress was an ingredient in the present climate of opinion.

Under the circumstances, one might wonder whether a history of Underhill's intellectual odyssey has anything to offer in the present day, apart from its intrinsic interest. The late British-American historian and intellectual, Tony Judt, whose work would have provided Underhill ample material for a file stuffed with notes and clippings if he had been a contemporary, perceived a change of outlook in the present very like a new climate of opinion, but which he called a new "paradigm." The language of the minimal state had become so pervasive, he thought, that it was difficult to find an acceptable discourse for the advocacy of social democratic ideas: "Our problem is not what to do; it is how to talk about it."⁵ Yet, the barriers presented by paradigm shifts and new climates of opinion can be exaggerated. The continuity of Underhill's idea of progress was not only with his nineteenth-century predecessors but with the eighteenth-century Enlightenment, as well. Indeed, the figure of the intellectual was a descendant of the *philosophe*, and the polemical use of wit, irony, and irreverence was common to them both. Underhill's moral outrage at the refusal of governments to expand the limits of state action in response to the conditions of the Great Depression has its counterpart in contemporary anger over the expanding income gap between rich and poor, after decades during which that gap had begun to close, to no small extent because of the "Keynesian revolution" and collective bargaining. Human beings, as Judt noted, citing Adam Smith's theory of moral sentiments, instinctively believe that selfishness is wrong, and respond to appeals to their better natures – at least some of the time.

Borrowing from Underhill's own philosophy of history, we might take three lessons from his life and thought. One is the necessity for frank discussion among those who share common values and interests, and for toleration of disagreement within a broad definition of those values and interests. Candour risks division, but it also offers the possibility of deepening understanding. The relationship between the CCF-NDP and the Liberal party has been historically dysfunctional, an undeniable thread of continuity from Underhill's time to ours. Party hierarchies, organizations, and cultures have become entrenched in their adversarial postures, exacerbated by imbalances in power. When the Liberals have been ahead, they have made little effort to reach out to the NDP; when, after the election of 2011, their positions were reversed, the NDP leadership followed suit. Meanwhile, on what we might think was potentially the level of ideas, leading Liberals in the former case counted former NDPers in their ranks (Bob Rae, Ujjal Dosanjh, John McCallum), while in the latter case the NDP leader (Thomas Mulcair) is a former Liberal. Do they not share common values and interests? At the national level, Underhill came to realize that the same frank discussion and tolerance was required between English-speaking and French-speaking Canadians. His example, it is true, might lead us to despair of ideas playing any role in Canadian politics, though it might also persuade us of the merits of a mediating Mackenzie King figure.

A second lesson we might learn from him is the need to temper expectations, and to consider the practicalities of any program we might wish to adopt. Social democracy, with its compromises and moderation, is notoriously boring as a political ideology, and those countries that have adopted it in any significant degree are themselves less than exciting – Sweden, Norway, Denmark, to name the most obvious examples. Canada is a candidate for inclusion, both on the grounds of many policies implemented during the twentieth century, provincially and federally, and of the boredom it induces in many outside observers, not to mention its own citizens. This alone should be grounds for recognizing the virtues of dullness, to which one might add that pragmatism was among the leading values recommended by Judt, desperately seeking escape from the ideological obsessions of twenty-first-century American politics. Another American historian, James Kloppenberg, whose work would also have found a place in Underhill's files, has argued that the unifying theme of social democracy and progressivism on both sides of the Atlantic was an uncertainty about solutions, which instilled a suspicion of absolutism and encouraged moderation, pragmatism, and open-mindedness.[6] That is, any renaissance of social democratic ideas, or the emergence of some new, similar construct, must accept the need to justify programs on the grounds of whether they are workable, affordable, and sustainable. This goes for the reform of taxation as well, and for policies seeking to redistribute income, which must be shown to have a general benefit, as they did in the period of growing prosperity and stability from the end of the Second World War to the 1970s.

Any proposals of this kind will be contested on the political right and questioned by many who will think that their comfort and well-being have been achieved by their own efforts alone. Purportedly practical objections will be raised – "I am an economist" – when the real issue is the kind of society that one is seeking to build. Here is the third lesson Underhill might teach us. Practicality is not enough. Those who come together must decide on what ends they believe the state ought to serve, since these will determine what practical programs they will try to implement. And since the advancement of the common good entails the containment of individual appetites, they must also decide what demands will have to be made of citizens. In trying to identify these ends, and to generate a wider public debate about them, Underhill's courage might serve as a model to be followed. Judt, a man of no small courage himself, cautioned against blaming "the system," which too easily frees us of the obligation to debate means, but he had no doubt that ends come first, and that "the disposition to disagree, to reject and to dissent – however irritating it may be when taken to extremes – is the very lifeblood of an open society."[7] Underhill lived up to this necessary ideal throughout his adult life, promoting and defending his ideas about Canadian nationhood, the role of the state, and the practice of history. This involved him, inescapably, in a debate that was ethical as well as practical, which remains a necessity in the present.

Underhill sometimes joked, as he neared the end of his life, about the instructions Thomas Jefferson had left in his will that his epitaph state that he had been the author of the Declaration of Independence and the Virginia Statute for Religious Freedom, and that he had founded the University of Virginia – nothing about having served two terms as president of the United States. This appealed to Underhill's own sense of priorities, and he thought he would leave his own instructions, to the effect that it be inscribed in his epitaph that he had drafted the Regina Manifesto. After further consideration, however, he decided that the Manifesto had not been the world-changing document that the Declaration had been, after all, and decided against it.[8] We might think today, admittedly to the neglect of Underhill's sense of humour, that Judt's words would better suit the purpose.

Notes

ABBREVIATIONS

CF   *Canadian Forum*
CHAR   Canadian Historical Association, *Annual Report*
ISCL   Frank H. Underhill, *In Search of Canadian Liberalism*,
              intro. Kenneth C. Dewar (Toronto: Oxford
              University Press, 2013 [Macmillan, 1960])
LAC   Library and Archives Canada
OP   Office of the President
SP   Francis Reginald Scott Papers
UP   Frank Hawkins Underhill Papers
UTA   University of Toronto Archives

PROLOGUE

1 Stephen T. Leonard, "Introduction: A Genealogy of the Politicized Intellectual," in *Intellectuals and Public Life: Between Radicalism and Reform*, eds Leon Fink, Stephen T. Leonard, and Donald M. Reid (Ithaca: Cornell University Press, 1996), 10; and Jane Burbank, "Were the Russian *Intelligenty* Organic Intellectuals?," in ibid., 97–100.

2 Woodsworth to Underhill, 26 April 1929, vol. 9, UP, LAC; see Michiel Horn, *The League for Social Reconstruction: Intellectual Origins of the Democratic Left in Canada 1930–1942* (Toronto: University of Toronto Press, 1980), 19.

3 See, for example, A.B. McKillop, *A Disciplined Intelligence: Critical Inquiry and Canadian Culture in the Victorian Era* (Montreal:

McGill-Queen's University Press, 1979) and Ian Ross Robertson, *Sir Andrew Macphail: The Life and Legacy of a Canadian Man of Letters* (Montreal: McGill-Queen's University Press, 2008).

4 Stefan Collini, "Introduction: The Question of Intellectuals," in *Absent Minds: Intellectuals in Britain* (Oxford: Oxford University Press, 2006), 1–12; see also Kenneth C. Dewar, "Frank Underhill: Intellectual in Search of a Role," *Underhill Review* (Fall 2008), http://www.carleton.ca/underhillreview.

5 Speech of Frank H. Underhill at 80th birthday dinner, Rideau Club, Ottawa, 26 November 1969, p. 12, vol. 24, UP, LAC.

6 Peter Clarke, *Liberals and Social Democrats* (Cambridge: Cambridge University Press, 1978); Stefan Collini, *Liberalism and Sociology: L.T. Hobhouse and Political Argument in England, 1880–1914* (Cambridge and New York: Cambridge University Press, 1979).

7 Underhill to Pearson, 20 January 1958, vol. 13, UP, LAC.

8 Kenneth McNaught, "Frank Underhill: A Personal Interpretation," *Queen's Quarterly* 79 (Summer 1972): 127–35.

9 Stefan Collini, *Public Moralists: Political Thought and Intellectual Life in Britain 1850–1930* (Oxford: Clarendon Press, 1991), 185.

10 "Bibliography of the Writings of Frank H. Underhill," in *On Canada: Essays in Honour of Frank H. Underhill*, ed. Norman Penlington (Toronto: University of Toronto Press, 1971), 131–92.

11 Kenneth C. Dewar, *Charles Clarke, Pen and Ink Warrior* (Montreal and Kingston: McGill-Queen's University Press, 2002).

12 See, for example, Barry Ferguson, *Remaking Liberalism: The Intellectual Legacy of O.D. Skelton, W.C. Clark, and W.A. Mackintosh, 1890–1925* (Montreal and Kingston: McGill-Queen's University Press, 1993) and Doug Owram, *The Government Generation: Canadian Intellectuals and the State 1900–1945* (Toronto: University of Toronto Press, 1986).

CHAPTER ONE

1 Kenneth N. Bell to G.M. Wrong, 17 December [1911], box 0001, George MacKinnon Wrong Family Papers, UTA.

2 Bell to Wrong, 21 November [1912], box 0001, George MacKinnon Wrong Family Papers, UTA.

3 Speech of Frank H. Underhill at 80th birthday dinner, Rideau Club, Ottawa, 26 November 1969, vol. 24, UP, LAC (henceforth 80th birthday speech).

4 George Steiner, *In Bluebeard's Castle: Some Notes towards the Re-definition of Culture* (London: Faber, 1971), 13.

5 Asa Briggs, ed., *The Nineteenth Century: The Contradictions of Progress* (London: Thames and Hudson, 1970), 38, quoting British historian G.M. Young.

6 W.D. Meikle, "F.H. Underhill Interviews, 1967," vol. 95, UP, LAC.

7 University of Toronto Class and Prize Lists, 1911, Faculty of Arts, vol. 40, UP, LAC.

8 "Hobbes' Leviathan," Writings – Papers – University of Toronto, vol. 17, UP, LAC; Elizabeth Wallace to Underhill, 30 April 1960, vol. 15, UP, LAC.

9 "Burke and Hobbes as Guides to Modern Democracy," vol. 17, UP, LAC.

10 "Hobbes' Leviathan."

11 Paul Heilker, *The Essay: Theory and Pedagogy for an Active Form* (Urbana, IL: National Council of Teachers of English, 1996), 2; Kenneth C. Dewar, "Frank Underhill: The Historian as Essayist," *The Underhill Review* (Fall 2007), http://www.carleton.ca/underhillreview.

12 80th birthday speech.

13 "Burke and Hobbes."

14 "John Stuart Mill," vol. 17, UP, LAC.

15 George Dangerfield, *The Strange Death of Liberal England* (New York: Capricorn Books, 1961 [1935]).

16 "Commission Government in Cities," vol. 17, UP, LAC.

17 "Bernard Shaw [1915?]," vol. 17, UP, LAC.

18 Underhill to Wrong, 2 February 1912, George MacKinnon Wrong Family Papers, UTA.

19 Notebooks, University Career – Balliol College, vol. 89, UP, LAC.

20 L.T. Hobhouse, *Liberalism and Other Writings*, ed. James Meadowcroft (Cambridge: Cambridge University Press, 1994).

21 Peter Clarke, *Liberals and Social Democrats* (Cambridge: Cambridge University Press, 1978), 65; Stefan Collini, *Liberalism and Sociology: L.T. Hobhouse and Political Argument in England, 1880–1914* (Cambridge: Cambridge University Press, 1979), 79, 98.

22 "History of English Trade Unionism" and "Doctrinaire Imperialism," Lectures – Papers, Balliol and Saskatchewan, vol. 17, UP, LAC.

23 James Tait to Underhill, 29 August 1913; Lindsay to Underhill, 14 September 1913, vol. 2, UP, LAC.

24 Milner to Underhill, 20 December 1913, vol. 2, UP, LAC.

25 Underhill to mother, 18 October 1914, 10 February 1915, vol. 2, U P, L A C.
26 Underhill to mother, 5 November 1914, 23 January 1915, vol. 2, U P, L A C; Frank H. Underhill, "What, Then, Is the Manitoban, This New Man, or This Almost Chosen People," *Historical Papers* (Canadian Historical Association) 5 (1970): 37.
27 "German Political Theory – Treitschke (1915)," Writings – Lectures, University of Saskatchewan, vol. 17, U P, L A C.
28 "Imperial Architecture," *The Sheaf* 3, no. 5 (March 1915), http://scaa.usask.ca/gallery/sheaf.
29 Underhill to mother, 4 December and 13 December 1915, 27 January 1916, July 1916, vol. 16, U P, L A C.
30 Ibid., July 1916.
31 Underhill to mother, 8 April 1917 and 23 March 1918; see also Hertfordshire Regiment, War Diary, March 1918, http://bedfordregiment.org.uk/Hertsrgt/1stherts1918diary.html.
32 Diaries, 15 October 1916, 23 December 1916, 1 March 1917, vol. 91, U P, L A C.
33 Diaries, 6 October 1917.
34 Diaries, 10 October, 21 October, 29–30 October 1917.
35 Diaries, 1–3 November 1917, 24 May 1918.
36 Tim Cook, "From Destruction to Construction: The Khaki University of Canada, 1917–1919," *Journal of Canadian Studies* 37, no. 1 (Spring 2002): 128.

CHAPTER TWO

1 R. Douglas Francis, *Frank H. Underhill: Intellectual Provocateur* (Toronto: University of Toronto Press, 1986), 53; see also Shirley Spafford, *No Ordinary Academics: Economics and Political Science at the University of Saskatchewan, 1910–1960* (Toronto: University of Toronto Press, 2000), ch. 6, "A Natural Minoritarian," 92–111.
2 "The New Europe," Writings – Lectures, University of Saskatchewan, vol. 17, U P, L A C.
3 James Kloppenberg, *Uncertain Victory: Social Democracy and Progressivism in European and American Thought, 1870–1920* (New York: Oxford University Press, 1986), 299–300.
4 Underhill to Thaddeus, 22 March 1926, vol. 2, U P, L A C; see also Walter Lippmann, file 953a, vol. 78, U P, L A C.

5 Quoted in Peter Clarke, *Liberals and Social Democrats* (Cambridge: Cambridge University Press, 1978), 135–6; Charles Forcey, *The Crossroads of Liberalism: Croly, Weyl, Lippmann, and the Progressive Era, 1900–1925* (New York: Oxford University Press, 1961), 100–1.

6 Clarke, *Liberals and Social Democrats*, 146, 149; Lippmann lecture notes, 29 November 1967, Walter Lippmann, file 953a, vol. 78, UP, LAC.

7 Peter Gay, *Modernism: The Lure of Heresy from Baudelaire to Beckett and Beyond* (NY: W.W. Norton, 2008).

8 "The Canadian Forces in the War," in *The Empire at War*, vol. 2, ed. Sir Charles Lucas (London: Oxford University Press, 1923), 79–287.

9 Quoted in Francis, *Underhill*, 49.

10 Tim Cook, *Clio's Warriors: Canadian Historians and the Writing of the World Wars* (Vancouver: University of British Columbia Press, 2006), 47.

11 Richard Preston, "Underhill on the Empire and Commonwealth" (unpublished manuscript, 1970), p. 3, Writings 1971, vol. 24, UP, LAC.

12 "Canadian Forces in the War," 100, 180, 206, 286.

13 "Canada's National Status," Writings – Speeches 1920s, vol. 17, UP, LAC.

14 "November 11, 1925," Writings – Various Dates, vol. 17, UP, LAC.

15 "On Political Education," Writings – Public Speeches for 1920s, vol. 17, UP, LAC.

16 Untitled (1924), Writings – Speeches 1920s, vol. 17, UP, LAC; "Some Aspects of the History of Parties in Canada" (1925), vol. 17, UP, LAC.

17 [Notes], *Globe* 1857–67, vols 49–50, files 388c–398b.

18 W.L. Morton, *The Progressive Party in Canada* (Toronto: University of Toronto Press, 1967 [1950]), 194, 200; David Laycock, *Populism and Democratic Thought in the Canadian Prairies, 1910–1945* (Toronto: University of Toronto Press, 1990), 32–68.

19 Untitled (1925), Writings – Speeches 1920s, vol. 17, UP, LAC.

20 "Some Aspects of Upper Canadian Radical Opinion in the Decade before Confederation," CHAR 6 (1927): 46–61, reprinted in *ISCL*, 43–67.

21 R.G. Trotter, "British Finance and Confederation," CHAR 6 (1927): 89–96; W.N. Sage, "Some Aspects of the Frontier in Canadian History," CHAR 7 (1928): 62–72.

22 "Upper Canadian Radical Opinion," 61.

23 "July 1, 1927," Writings 1927, vol. 17, UP, LAC.

24 "July 1, 1927," and "The Dominion of Canada after 60 Years" [30 June 1927], Writings 1927, vol. 17, UP, LAC.

25 Wrong to Underhill, 1 February 1927, and draft reply, 20 February 1927, vol. 2, UP, LAC; Falconer to Underhill, 3 May 1927, vol. 1, UP, LAC.

26 Wrong to Underhill, 21 March 1923, vol. 1, UP, LAC; Francis, *Underhill*, 74, 191n20; A.B. McKillop, *Matters of Mind: The University in Ontario, 1791–1951* (Toronto: University of Toronto Press, 1994), 379.

27 Donald Wright, *The Professionalization of History in English Canada* (Toronto: University of Toronto Press, 2005), 71.

28 Ibid., 54, 68, 71–2.

29 Ibid., 63; Underhill to Walter Murray, 9 January 1926, vol. 1, UP, LAC; History 1791–1839, vol. 51, UP, LAC.

30 "Toronto and Montreal" [possibly 1928], Writings – Undated, vol. 16, UP, LAC.

31 Francis, *Underhill*, 73–5; William Duncan Meikle, "And Gladly Teach: G.M. Wrong and the Department of History at the University of Toronto" (PhD thesis, Michigan State University, 1977), 166–81, 249–65; John English, *Shadow of Heaven: The Life of Lester Pearson*, vol. 1, *1897–1948* (London: Vintage, 1990), 133–5.

32 CF 1 (October 1920), 3; Ann Stephenson Cowan, "*The Canadian Forum* 1920–1950: An Historical Study in Canadian Literary Theory and Practice" (MA thesis, Carleton University, 1974), 24–6.

33 Graham Carr, "Design as Content: Foreign Influences and the Identity of English-Canadian Intellectual Magazines, 1919–1939," *American Review of Canadian Studies* 18, no. 2 (1988): 186.

34 Northrop Frye, "Rear View Crystal Ball," CF 50 (April–May 1970): 54.

35 Sandra Djwa, "The *Canadian Forum*: Literary Catalyst," *Studies in Canadian Literature* 1, no. 1 (1976): 8.

36 Allen Mills, "*The Canadian Forum* and Socialism, 1920–1934," *Journal of Canadian Studies* 13, no. 4 (Winter 1978–79): 11–13.

37 Underhill, review of *The Growth of Canadian National Feeling*, by W. Stewart Wallace, CF 8 (December 1927): 465–6.

38 Fred Landon to Underhill, 15 June 1928, vol. 5, UP, LAC; R.A. MacKay to Underhill, 19 March 1930, vol. 6; Woodsworth to Underhill, 26 April 1929, vol. 9; Dafoe to Underhill, 5 May 1931,

vol. 16. See Margaret Prang, "F.H.U. of *The Canadian Forum*," in
On Canada: Essays in Honour of Frank H. Underhill, ed. Norman
Penlington (Toronto: University of Toronto Press, 1971), 3–23.

39 *CF* 11 (October 1930): 12.

40 *CF* 11 (July 1931): 369.

41 "The League of Nations," *Modern Education* (October 1925): 10,
Writings – 1925 League of Nations, vol. 17, UP, LAC.

42 "The International Labor Organization" (typescript), p. 6, Writings –
1925 League of Nations, vol. 17, UP, LAC.

43 *CF* 10 (March 1930): 200–2; "Canada's Relations with the Empire as
Seen by the Toronto *Globe*, 1857–1867," *Canadian Historical Review*
10 (June 1929): 106–28.

44 O Canada, *CF* 10 (March 1930): 200–2; "Canada's National Status,"
CF 9 (January 1929): 120.

45 *CF* 9 (May 1929): 270.

46 *CF* 10 (November 1930): 52.

47 Ibid. and 9 (May 1929): 71.

48 Quoted in Francis, *Underhill*, 78.

49 Quoted in Martin L. Friedland, *The University of Toronto: A History*
(Toronto: University of Toronto Press, 2002), 348.

50 Francis, *Underhill*, 79–80; McKillop, *Matters of Mind*, 380.

51 "Canadian and American History – and Historians," *CF* 8 (June
1928): 685–8; see also O Canada, *CF* 10 (January 1930): 115.

52 "Musings without Method" [1929], Writings – Various Dates, vol. 17,
UP, LAC.

53 *CF* 9 (July 1929): 340–1.

54 Prang, "F.H.U.," 10.

55 *CF* 11 (October 1930): 27.

CHAPTER THREE

1 Lewis Coser, *Men of Ideas: A Sociologist's View* (New York: The Free
Press, 1965).

2 Herbert R. Lottman, *The Left Bank: Writers, Artists, and Politics from
the Popular Front to the Cold War* (Chicago: University of Chicago
Press, 1982), 17.

3 Underhill to Scott, 29 November 1931, vol. 17, SP, LAC.

4 *CF* 10 (October 1929): 10; see also "The Institute of Politics,"
Writings 1929, vol. 17; Duguit, vol. 25, file 17; Sir Paul Vinogradoff,
vol. 27, file 69, UP, LAC.

5 *The Race Question in Canada* was originally published as *Le Canada, les deux races: problèmes politiques contemporain* (Paris: Librairie Armand Colin, 1906). Underhill later edited and introduced it for the Carleton Library Series, No. 29 (Toronto: McClelland and Stewart, 1966).

6 F.W. Watt, "Climate of Unrest: Periodicals in the Twenties and Thirties," *Canadian Literature* 12 (Spring 1962): 19.

7 Scott, Autobiographical, vol. 81, file 3, S P, L A C.

8 Sandra Djwa, *The Politics of the Imagination: A Life of F.R. Scott* (Toronto: McClelland and Stewart, 1987), 51–2, 82–94, 127–8; see also Marlene Shore, "'Overtures of an Era Being Born' F.R. Scott: Cultural Nationalism and Social Criticism 1925–1939," *Journal of Canadian Studies* 15, no. 4 (Winter 1980–81): 32–3.

9 Scott, "New Poems for Old, I and II," C F 11 (May 1931): 297, and (June 1931): 338. On the US as the embodiment of modernity in the 1920s, see Damien-Claude Bélanger, *Prejudice and Pride: Canadian Intellectuals Confront the United States, 1891–1945* (Toronto: University of Toronto Press, 2011), 32–3.

10 "The League for Social Reconstruction," C F 12 (April 1932): 249; see also Djwa, *Politics of the Imagination*, 131.

11 Kenneth Norrie and Douglas Owram, *A History of the Canadian Economy*, 2nd ed. (Toronto: Harcourt Brace, 1996), 353–61, 368–72.

12 Scott to Underhill, 7 March 1932, vol. 16, U P, L A C.

13 Djwa, *Politics of the Imagination*, 130; Michiel Horn, *The League for Social Reconstruction: Intellectual Origins of the Democratic Left in Canada, 1930–1942* (Toronto: University of Toronto Press, 1980), 18.

14 Scott, "The Trial of the Toronto Communists," *Queen's Quarterly* 39 (1932): 512–27, reprinted in Frank R. Scott, *Essays on the Constitution: Aspects of Canadian Law and Politics* (Toronto: University of Toronto Press, 1977), 49–59.

15 Michiel Horn, "'Free Speech within the Law': The Letter of the Sixty-Eight Toronto Professors, 1931," *Ontario History* 72 (March 1980): 27, 32; Free Speech – The Letter of the 68, 1931, vol. 49, U P, L A C; see also A.B. McKillop, *Matters of Mind: The University in Ontario, 1791–1951* (Toronto: University of Toronto Press, 1994), 381–4.

16 Horn, "Free Speech," 33.

17 "The Intellectual Capital of Canada," C F 11 (March 1931): 211.

18 C F 12 (December 1931): 93.

19 Horn, *League for Social Reconstruction*, Appendix 1, The LSR Manifesto, 219–20.
20 Underhill to Scott, 18 December 1931, vol. 17 SP, LAC.
21 Underhill to Rogers, 14 January 1932 and reply, 18 January 1932, vol. 7, UP, LAC.
22 Underhill to Scott, 7 April 1932, vol. 17, SP, LAC.
23 Horn, *League for Social Reconstruction*, Appendix 1, 221–2.
24 Quoted in James Kloppenberg, *Uncertain Victory: Social Democracy and Progressivism in European and American Thought, 1870–1920* (New York: Oxford University Press, 1986), 405.
25 "Bentham and Benthamism," *Queen's Quarterly* 39 (November 1932): 658–68; quoted passages at 658, 665, 667, 668.
26 Walter Young, *The Anatomy of a Party: The National CCF 1932–61* (Toronto: University of Toronto Press, 1969), 28.
27 Underhill to Woodsworth, 2 May 1933; Underhill to Woodsworth, 29 July 1934, and reply, 2 August 1934, vol. 16, UP, LAC.
28 Underhill to Scott, 30 August 1932, vol. 17, SP, LAC.
29 Scott to A.D. MacDonald, St Francis Xavier University Extension Department, 7 October 1932, vol. 17, SP, LAC.
30 Underhill to Scott, 30 August 1932, vol. 7, SP, LAC; Horn, *League for Social Reconstruction*, 37–40.
31 Scott to Underhill, 20 October 1932, SP, LAC.
32 Michiel Horn, "Frank Underhill's Early Drafts of the Regina Manifesto 1933," *Canadian Historical Review* 54, no. 4 (December 1973): 393–418.
33 Horn, *League for Social Reconstruction*, 46.
34 "The Function of the Historian," CF 12 (June 1932): 344–5.
35 "Goldwin Smith," *University of Toronto Quarterly* 2 (April 1933): 285–309, reprinted in ISCL, 85–103, quoted passages at 85, 90, 96.
36 "The Party System in Canada," *Papers and Proceedings* of the Canadian Political Science Association, vol. 4 (1932), reprinted in ISCL, quoted at 165.
37 Ibid., 171.
38 C.A. Beard, vol. 76, file 890b, UP, LAC.
39 "The Development of National Parties in Canada," *Canadian Historical Review* 16 (December 1935): 367–87; reprinted in ISCL, 21–42, Madison quoted at 21, Smith at 37.
40 League for Social Reconstruction Research Committee, *Social Planning for Canada* (Toronto: Thomas Nelson, 1935), 464–88.

41 "The Conception of a National Interest," *Canadian Journal of Economics and Political Science* 1 (1935): 396–408, reprinted in ISCL, 172–82; quotations at 175, 176, and 179.

42 Ibid., 180–1.

43 H.A. Innis, "'For the People,'" *University of Toronto Quarterly* 5 (January 1936): 285, 287.

44 "On Professors and Politics," CF 15 (March 1936): 6–7, reprinted in ISCL, 107–9.

45 Spry to Underhill, 22 October 1929, vol. 8; Claxton to Underhill, 19 February 1931, vol. 3; Martin to Underhill, 4 June 1931, vol. 6, UP, LAC.

46 Quoted in Kenneth C. Dewar, "F.H. Underhill and the Making of 'The Intellectual'," *History of Intellectual Culture* 8, no. 1 (2008–09), http://www.ucalgary.ca/hic; A.B. McKillop, *A Critical Spirit: The Thought of William Dawson LeSueur*, Carleton Library No. 104 (Toronto: McClelland and Stewart, 1977).

47 "The Institute of Politics" (typescript), 1–2, Writings 1929, vol. 17, UP, LAC.

48 Underhill Bibliography, "Commerce Courses and the Arts Faculty," vol. 17, UP, LAC; reprinted from *The University of Toronto Monthly* (October 1930) [2, 3]; see Donald Wright, *The Professionalization of History in English Canada* (Toronto: University of Toronto Press, 2005), 105, 117.

49 CF 12 (February 1932): 172–3, 196.

50 Scott to Cassidy, 22 February 1935, and reply, 7 March 1935, League for Social Reconstruction, Harry Morris Cassidy Papers, box 071, UTA.

51 Scott to Underhill, 6 December 1935, and reply, 24 January 1936, F.R. Scott Correspondence, vol. 16, UP, LAC; "Beatty and the University Reds," CF 15 (December 1935): 385; Horn, *League for Social Reconstruction*, 189–90; see also Sir Edward Beatty, "Freedom and the Universities," *Queen's Quarterly* 44 (Winter 1937/38): 463–71.

52 Hugh R. Dent to Underhill, 14 October 1932, and reply, 5 November 1932; Dent to Underhill, 11 January 1934, vol. 4, UP, LAC.

53 Underhill to Hugh Keenleyside, 3 November 1935, vol. 16, UP, LAC.

54 Underhill to Scott, 27 April 1936; Godfrey to Scott, 19 May 1936; Grube to Scott, 2 May 1936, vol. 7, SP, LAC.

55 McNaught to Underhill, 7 May 1936 (copies to G.M.A. Grube and Eric Havelock), vol. 16, UP, LAC.

56 Mark Farrell to [Helen] Marsh, 22 January 1937, enclosing Memorandum by Farrell, vol. 7, S P, L A C.

57 Scott to Underhill, 26 February 1937; Underhill to Scott, 24 March 1937, vol. 7, S P, L A C.

58 Humphrey Carver, *Compassionate Landscape* (Toronto: University of Toronto Press, 1975), 44.

59 Earle Birney, *Spreading Time: Remarks on Canadian Writing and Writers 1904–1949* (Montreal: Véhicule Press, 1989 [1980]), 29, 37–8.

60 Kenneth McNaught, *Conscience and History: A Memoir* (Toronto: University of Toronto Press, 1999), 17.

61 Underhill to Scott, 30 October 1937, and reply, 13 November 1937, vol. 18, S P, L A C; Underhill to Scott, 18 January 1938, vol. 7, S P, L A C.

CHAPTER FOUR

1 Michiel Horn, *Academic Freedom in Canada: A History* (Toronto: University of Toronto Press, 1999), 96–7.

2 Wrong to Underhill, 7 December 1933, vol. 9, U P, L A C.

3 Quoted in Horn, *Academic Freedom*, 97.

4 R. Douglas Francis, *Frank H. Underhill: Intellectual Provocateur* (Toronto: University of Toronto Press, 1986), 97.

5 "Foreign Policy," in League for Social Reconstruction Research Committee, *Social Planning for Canada* (Toronto: Thomas Nelson, 1935), 522.

6 R.A. MacKay and E.B. Rogers, *Canada Looks Abroad* (Toronto: Oxford University Press, 1938), 269.

7 O Canada, C F 9 (July 1929): 340–1.

8 Francis, *Underhill*, 109–10; Horn, *Academic Freedom*, 119–20.

9 Statement Regarding Professor Frank Underhill, April 1939, President's Correspondence Files 1939–41, A72-0033/001 (01), O P, U T A.

10 Statement Regarding Professor Frank Underhill; Underhill to Cody, 19 April 1939, President's Correspondence Files 1939–41, A72-0033/001 (03), O P, U T A.

11 Martin to Cody, 19 April 1939, President's Correspondence Files 1939–41, A72-0033/001 (03), O P, U T A; Underhill to Scott, 9 May 1939, vol. 23; Underhill to Scott, 6 October 1939, vol. 7, S P, L A C.

12 Underhill to Cody, 4 September 1940 (typescript attached), A72-0033/001 (03), OP, UTA; see also Frank H. Underhill, "North American Front," CF 20 (September 1940): 166–7.

13 Quoted in Francis, *Underhill*, 116–17; see also Horn, *Academic Freedom*, 154–55, and A.B. McKillop, *Matters of Mind: The University in Ontario, 1791–1951* (Toronto: University of Toronto Press, 1994), 541–3.

14 Underhill to Scott, 19 September 1940, vol. 29, reel 1280, SP, LAC.

15 Underhill to Rev. D. Bruce Macdonald, chairman, Board of Governors, 8 January 1941, A72-0033/001 (01), OP, UTA.

16 Stanley to Cody, 26 February 1941, A72-0033/001 (01), OP, UTA.

17 Brebner to Innis, 10 January (forwarded), Keenleyside to Cody, 15 January 1941, and Cody to V. Even Gray, 15 January 1941, A72-0033/001 (01); Cody to Clifford Sifton, 13 January 1941, A72-0033/001 (02), OP, UTA.

18 Writings 1939, 1940, 1941, vol. 19, UP, LAC. These files are stuffed with clippings about the affair.

19 Creighton to Scott, 10 January 1941, and J. King Gordon to Scott, 10 January 1941, vol. 29, SP, LAC.

20 Horn, *Academic Freedom*, 162–4; Francis, *Underhill*, 126–7; D.C. Masters, *Henry John Cody: An Outstanding Life* (Toronto: Dundurn Press, 1995), 267–8.

21 Underhill to Scott, 4 January 1941 and 15 January 1941, "Some Account of Recent Strange Happenings in the University of Toronto" (Confidential), vol. 29, reel 1280, SP, LAC.

22 Quoted in Francis, *Underhill*, 127.

23 Michiel Horn, *The League for Social Reconstruction: Intellectual Origins of the Democratic Left in Canada, 1930–1942* (Toronto: University of Toronto Press, 1980), 162; Walter Young, *The Anatomy of a Party: The National CCF 1932–61* (Toronto: University of Toronto Press, 1969), 92–4; James Naylor, "Pacifism or Anti-Imperialism? The CCF Response to the Outbreak of World War II," *Journal of the Canadian Historical Association* 8 (1997): 236.

24 "The LSR: Its Economic, Political, and Social Context," Conference Proceedings, 17–18 October 1980, cassette 5B, UTA.

25 Horn, *League for Social Reconstruction*, 164–5; Francis, *Underhill*, 129–30.

26 "Peace Aims," CF 19 (October 1939): 207–9.

27 "Foreign Policy," in L S R Research Committee, *Social Planning for Canada* (Toronto: Thomas Nelson, 1935), 518; "Canada and the Last War," in *Canada in Peace and War; Eight Studies in National Trends since 1914*, ed. Chester Martin (London and New York: Oxford University Press, 1941), 130, 134; Francis, *Underhill*, 130–2.

28 Underhill to Scott, 22 April 1941, and reply, 26 April 1941, vol. 18, S P, L A C.

29 Horn, *League for Social Reconstruction*, 170–2.

30 "Meighen 1942," vol. 54, files 499a-b, U P, L A C; Francis, *Underhill*, 134–5.

31 "Edward Blake, the Supreme Court Act, and the Appeal to the Privy Council, 1875–76," *Canadian Historical Review* 19 (September 1938): 245–62; "Edward Blake, the Liberal Party, and Unrestricted Reciprocity," C H A R 18 (1939): 133–41; "Laurier and Blake, 1882–1891," *Canadian Historical Review* 20 (December 1939): 392–408; "Edward Blake and Canadian Liberal Nationalism," in *Essays in Canadian History; Presented to George M. Wrong for his Eightieth Birthday*, ed. Ralph Flenley (Toronto: Macmillan, 1939), 132–53.

32 "The Political Ideas of the Upper Canada Reformers, 1867–1878," C H A R 21 (1942): 104–15, reprinted in *I S C L*, 68–84; "Laurier and Blake, 1891–2," *Canadian Historical Review* 24 (June 1943): 135–55.

33 "Edward Blake and Canadian Liberal Nationalism," 136, 147–8.

34 Ibid., 138, 140.

35 Ibid., 132, 147, 138–9, 148.

36 "Edward Blake, the Supreme Court Act," 249, 260–1.

37 "Laurier and Blake, 1882–1891," 393.

38 Edward Blake, the Liberal Party, and Unrestricted Reciprocity," 134, 140; see also Ben Forster and Jonathan Swainger, "Edward Blake," *Dictionary of Canadian Biography Online*, vol. 12, 1911–1920, http://www.biographi.ca/009004-119.01-e.php?&id_nbr=7213.

39 "Laurier and Blake, 1891–2," 149, 155.

40 "Political Ideas of the Upper Canada Reformers," in *I S C L*, 68.

41 "The Canadian Party System in Transition," *Canadian Journal of Economics and Political Science* 9 (August 1943): 300–16, quotation at 301; reprinted in *I S C L*, 192–202.

42 Ibid., 306, 309–12.

43 McNaught to Underhill, 5 May 1943 (enclosing Cassidy to McNaught, 27 April 1943), and reply, 7 May 1943, vol. 6, U P, L A C.

44 Underhill, interview by W.D. Meikle, 11 September 1968 (transcript), vol. 95, U P, L A C.

45 "Memorandum on the Canadian Forum," 27 November 1943, 9, vol. 40, file 279, U P, L A C; Godfrey to Scott, 9 November 1945, vol. 7, S P, L A C; Underhill to Scott, 27 January 1946, vol. 7, S P, L A C; Francis, *Underhill*, 141–2.

46 "J.S. Woodsworth," in *I S C L*, 163.

47 "John Morley," Writings 1945, vol. 19, and "Notes from His Writings," vol. 26, files 42a-c, U P, L A C; on Morley's individualism, see Peter Clarke, *Liberals and Social Democrats* (Cambridge: Cambridge University Press, 1978), 41.

48 "Some Reflections on the Liberal Tradition in Canada," C H A R 25 (1946): 5–17, reprinted in *I S C L*, 3–20, quotations at 4–5.

49 "The Social Scientist in the Modern World," C H A R 20 (1941): 83; see also A.R.M. Lower, "The Social Sciences in the Post-War World," *Canadian Historical Review* 22 (March 1941): 1–13.

50 "Some Reflections," in *I S C L*, 7, 8, 20.

51 Ibid., 13, 15.

52 "Random Remarks on Socialism and Freedom," C F 27 (August 1947): 110–11; reprinted in *I S C L*, 203–6.

53 G.M.A. Grube, "Socialism and Freedom," C F 27 (September 1947): 128–30.

54 Francis, *Underhill*, 51.

55 Stuart Garson to Underhill, 2 September 1947, vol. 4, U P, L A C.

56 Isaiah Berlin, "The Hedgehog and the Fox," in *Russian Thinkers* (Harmondsworth, England: Penguin Books, 1979 [1978]), 22–3.

CHAPTER FIVE

1 Underhill to Lester B. Pearson, 20 January 1958, vol. 13, U P, L A C.

2 "The Close of an Era: Twenty-Five Years of Mr. Mackenzie King," C F 24 (September 1944): 125–6; "Twenty-Five Years as Prime Minister," C F 26 (July 1946): 77–8; "Liberalism à la King," review of *Industry and Humanity*, by W.L. Mackenzie King, C F 27 (February 1948): 257–8.

3 "The End of the King Era, Part I," C F 28 (August 1948): 97–8; "The End of the King Era, Part II," C F 28 (September 1948): 121–1, 126–7.

4 "Concerning Mr. King," C F 30 (September 1950): 121–2, 125–7. These articles on King are all reprinted in *I S C L*, 114–41.

5 "Political Parties and Ideas," in *Canada*, ed. George W. Brown (Berkeley and Los Angeles: University of California Press, 1950), 331, 351–2.

6 "How to Vote," CF 33 (July 1953): 73, 76–7. Stewart Kinloch Dicks observed this transition in Underhill's analysis in 1961; see *The Evolution of Radicalism in the Work of F.H. Underhill* (master's thesis, University of Western Ontario, 1968), Ann Arbor: ProQuest/UMI, Publication No. MK02712, 162.

7 "Fabians and Fabianism, Part II," CF 26 (April 1946): 11.

8 R. Douglas Francis, *Frank H. Underhill: Intellectual Provocateur* (Toronto: University of Toronto Press, 1986), 150.

9 The story is told in Francis, *Underhill*, 149–53, and in greater detail in R. Douglas Francis, "The Ontario Woodsworth House Controversy: 1944–1954," *Ontario History* 71 (March 1979): 27–37; see also Dicks, *Evolution of Radicalism*, 47–67.

10 "Socialism after 50 Years," CCF 1953 [*sic*], vol. 45, UP, LAC.

11 Newsletter, 1 October 1951, vol. 45, UP, LAC.

12 Coldwell to Underhill, 6 January 1951 and 14 February 1952, vol. 16, UP, LAC.

13 Francis, "Ontario Woodsworth House," 32–3.

14 Dicks, *Evolution of Radicalism*, 60; Francis, *Underhill*, 153.

15 "Power Politics in the Ontario C.C.F.," CF 22 (April 1952): 7–8.

16 Damien-Claude Bélanger, *Prejudice and Pride: Canadian Intellectuals Confront the United States, 1891–1945* (Toronto: University of Toronto Press, 2011), 27.

17 Robert Bothwell, *Alliance and Illusion: Canada and the World, 1945–1984* (Vancouver: University of British Columbia Press, 2007), 47.

18 S.W. Bradford, "The CCF Failure in Foreign Policy," CF 30 (September 1950): 127–8; see also Kenneth McNaught, *Conscience and History: A Memoir* (Toronto: University of Toronto Press, 1999), 60–2.

19 "Canadian Socialism and World Politics," CF 30 (October 1950): 149–50.

20 For example, "Russia and the West," *International Journal* 2 (Autumn 1947): 338–43; "The Defence of Man: Philosophy and Politics," *International Journal* 4 (Winter 1948/49): 60–6; "Airstrip One – 1950," *International Journal* 5 (Winter 1949/50): 61–70.

21 "The Lights Go Out in Czechoslovakia," CF 28 (April 1948): 1.

22 "Arnold Toynbee, Metahistorian," review of *A Study of History*, by Arnold Toynbee, vols 1–6, *Canadian Historical Review* 32 (September

1951): 201–19; "The Toynbee of the 1950's," review of vols 7–10, *Canadian Historical Review* 36 (September 1955): 222–35.

23 "So Little for the Mind: Comments and Queries," *Transactions* (Royal Society of Canada) 48, series 3 (June 1954): 22; see also "Notes on the Massey Report," CF 31 (August 1951): 100–2, reprinted in *Our Sense of Identity: A Book of Canadian Essays*, ed. Malcolm Ross (Toronto: Ryerson Press, 1954), 33–9 and ISCL, 209–13; Kenneth C. Dewar, "Hilda Neatby and the Ends of Education," *Queen's Quarterly* 97 (Spring 1990): 36–51.

24 Neatby to Underhill, 29 January 1954 and 11 March 1955, vol. 6, UP, LAC.

25 Garson to Underhill, 13 January 1955 and reply, 18 January 1955, vol. 4, UP, LAC.

26 "Canadian Liberal Democracy in 1955," in ISCL, 227–42. See also Frank H. Underhill and G.V. Ferguson, *Press and Party in Canada: Issues of Freedom*, Chancellor Dunning Trust Lectures (Toronto: Ryerson Press, 1955).

27 Garson to Underhill, 7 February 1955, vol. 4, UP, LAC.

28 Francis, *Underhill*, 161.

29 Underhill to Dawson, 19 December 1934, and reply, 8 January 1935, vol. 4, UP, LAC.

30 Francis, *Underhill*, 162–3.

31 "The Revival of Conservatism in North America," *Transactions* (Royal Society of Canada) 52, series 3 (June 1958): 1, 3, 5.

32 Ibid., 17, 19; see Donald Creighton, "Presidential Address," CHAR 36 (1957), 1–12.

33 "The Winnipeg Declaration of the C.C.F.," *Globe and Mail*, 21 August 1956, reprinted in ISCL, 243–47.

34 "Canadian Liberal Democracy in 1955," 240–1.

35 Pearson to Underhill, 11 February 1958, vol. 13, UP, LAC.

36 Mitchell Sharp to Underhill, 12 May 1960, vol. 13, UP, LAC.

37 John English, *The Worldly Years: The Life of Lester Pearson*, vol. 2, 1949–1972 (Toronto: Knopf Canada, 1992), 209.

38 Tom Kent, *A Public Purpose: An Experience of Liberal Opposition and Canadian Government* (Montreal and Kingston: McGill-Queen's University Press, 1988), 79–89; P.E. Bryden, *Planners and Politicians: Liberal Politics and Social Policy, 1957–1968* (Montreal and Kingston: McGill-Queen's University Press, 1997), 55–64.

39 For a brief summary of these reports and their context, see Leonard
   Marsh, "Introduction" to *Report on Social Security for Canada*, with
   a new introduction by the author and a preface by Michael Bliss
   (Toronto: University of Toronto Press, 1975), xxiii–xxxi.

40 Robert Malcolm Campbell, *Grand Illusions: The Politics of the
   Keynesian Experience in Canada, 1945–1975* (Peterborough:
   Broadview Press, 1987), 197.

41 Francis, *Underhill*, 170; Mitchell Sharp, *Which Reminds Me … : A
   Memoir* (Toronto: University of Toronto Press, 1994), 91–2.

42 *In Search of Canadian Liberalism* (Toronto: Macmillan, 1960).

43 "Old Wine in New Bottles," review of *The New Party*, by Stanley
   Knowles, CF 41 (May 1961), 35–6.

44 T.W. Kent, *Social Policy for Canada: Towards a Philosophy of Social
   Security* (Ottawa: Policy Press, 1962), 39–50.

45 "New Canadian Frontier?," review of *Social Purpose for Canada*, ed.
   Michael Oliver, *Queen's Quarterly* 69 (Summer 1962): 294–301.

46 Underhill to Pearson, 29 April 1963, and reply, 6 May 1963, vol. 13,
   UP, LAC.

CHAPTER SIX

1 R. Douglas Francis, *Frank H. Underhill: Intellectual Provocateur*
   (Toronto: University of Toronto Press, 1986), 162.

2 Underhill to Mike Pearson, 7 August 1955, vol. 7, UP, LAC.

3 *Globe and Mail* 1957–71, vol. 11; *Toronto Star* 1962–67, vols. 14 and
   17, UP, LAC.

4 *American (Encyclopedia) Annual* 1957–71, vol. 10; *Encyclopedia
   Canadiana*, vol. 4; John E. Robbins to Underhill, 13 September 1956;
   World Book Encyclopedia 1963, vol. 15. All in UP, LAC.

5 Clinton Rossiter to Underhill, 25 March 1959, vol. 13; James M.
   Minifie to Underhill, 4 August 1961, vol. 12; George Grant to Underhill,
   25 August 1962, vol. 11; Hugh Keenleyside to Underhill, 1 March
   1962, vol. 12; Underhill to Tom Kent, n.d. [1957], vol. 12, UP, LAC.

6 Underhill to Tom Kent, 1 December 1958 and reply, 5 December
   1958, vol. 12; Underhill to W.A. MacIntosh, 6 December 1958, UP,
   LAC; Tom Kent, *A Public Purpose: An Experience of Liberal
   Opposition and Canadian Government* (Montreal and Kingston:
   McGill-Queen's University Press, 1988), 74–5.

7   "Ramsay Cook – J.W. Dafoe," Preliminary and Final Reports, 27 November and 18 December 1961, vol. 34; see also Canada Council, "Report on W.L. Morton – Request to Canada Council," 19 April 1968, vol. 10, UP, LAC.

8   "Was King Innocent or Statesman?," review of *In Defence of Canada,* vol. 2: *Appeasement and Rearmament,* by James Eayrs, *Globe Magazine,* 1 January 1966.

9   Multiple thick files of notes and cuttings for all of these authors are in vols 24–27, 34, 51, 76–79, UP, LAC.

10 Stanley Knowles, vol. 12, UP, LAC; Coldwell Fund, vol. 40, UP, LAC.

11 Charles G. Power to Underhill, 24 October 1960, vol. 13; John N. Turner to Underhill, Personal and Confidential, 29 September 1961, vol. 14, UP, LAC; John English, *The Worldly Years: The Life of Lester Pearson,* vol. 2: *1949–1972* (Toronto: Knopf Canada, 1992), 236.

12 Jean-Luc Pepin to Underhill, 22 February 1967, vol. 13; "What the Liberals Might Learn from the CCF-NDP," Writings - Undated, vol. 16, UP, LAC.

13 Francis, *Underhill,* 172–3.

14 John Gray to Underhill, 18 March 1955, vol. 6; Kildare Dobbs to Underhill, 28 September 1956, vol. 6; Dobbs to Underhill, 3 January 1957, vol. 12, UP, LAC.

15 Dobbs to Underhill, 5 September 1958; Underhill to Dobbs, 24 September 1958; Underhill to Dobbs, 12 November 1958; Dobbs to Underhill, 15 April 1959; Underhill to Dobbs, 25 November 1959. All in vol. 12, UP, LAC.

16 "Introduction," *ISCL*, ix–xiv.

17 Don McGillivray, "True Liberal Lacks Party Loyalty," *Winnipeg Tribune,* 22 October 1960; Robert Fulford, "The Professor in Politics," *Toronto Daily Star,* 26 October 1960; J.R. Mallory, review in *Canadian Journal of Economics and Political Science* 27 (August 1961): 388–9; Mason Wade, review in *American Historical Review* 67 (July 1962): 1073–5.

18 Bernard Trotter to Underhill, 18 January 1963; Underhill to Trotter, 20 January 1963, UP, LAC.

19 *The Image of Confederation* (Toronto: Canadian Broadcasting Corporation, 1964), 4.

20 Ibid., 9.

21 Ibid., 2, 70.

22 Ibid., 35, 39, 44, 47, 53.

23 Ibid., 60, 62, 64, 67.

24 Robert Fulford, *Toronto Star*, 4 June 1966.

25 *ISCL*, xiii.

26 A.R.M. Lower to Underhill, 2 January 1953, vol. 5, UP, LAC.

27 Francis, *Underhill*, 173; Wade, review, 1075.

28 Norman Penlington, ed., preface to *On Canada: Essays in Honour of Frank H. Underhill* (Toronto: University of Toronto Press, 1971), xi; Carl Berger, *The Writing of Canadian History: Aspects of English-Canadian Historical Writing: 1900–1970*, 2nd ed. (Toronto: University of Toronto Press, 1986 [1976]), 55, 84; *ISCL*, xi.

29 Francis, *Underhill*, 140.

30 "Edward Blake," in *Our Living Tradition: Seven Canadians*, ed. Claude T. Bissell (Toronto: University of Toronto Press, 1957), 3–28.

31 Blake manuscript, ch. 1, p. 8, vol. 65, file 689, UP, LAC.

32 Joseph Schull, *Edward Blake*, 2 vols (Toronto: Macmillan, 1975 and 1976); Ben Forster and Jonathan Swainger, "Edward Blake," *Dictionary of Canadian Biography Online*, vol. 12, 1911–1920, http://www.biographi.ca/009004-119.01-e.php?&id_nbr=7213.

33 "Edward Blake," in *Our Living Tradition*, 4.

34 Donald Creighton, "John A. Macdonald," in *Our Living Tradition*, 49, 51.

35 Underhill to A.W. Trueman, Canada Council, 19 June 1957, vol. 10; McClelland and Stewart file, vol. 12, UP, LAC.

36 Underhill, introduction to *The Race Question in Canada*, by André Siegfried, Carleton Library No. 29 (Toronto: McClelland and Stewart, 1966), 1, 8.

37 "Conservatism = Socialism = Anti-Americanism" (manuscript), review of *Lament for a Nation*, by George Grant, *Journal of Liberal Thought* 1 (Summer 1965), vol. 34, UP, LAC.

38 Norman Ward to Underhill, 24 March 1961, vol. 15, UP, LAC.

39 Underhill, foreword to the University League for Social Reform, *Nationalism in Canada*, ed. Peter Russell (Toronto: McGraw-Hill, 1966), xix.

40 "Canadian Intellectuals and Politics," Writings 1967 [1], vol. 24, UP, LAC, 1–28; H. Stuart Hughes, "Is the Intellectual Obsolete?" in *An Approach to Peace and Other Essays* (New York: Atheneum, 1962), 157–75.

41 John Gray to Underhill, 2 October 1961 and 10 September 1962, vol. 12, UP, LAC.

42 Speech of Frank H. Underhill at 80th birthday dinner, Rideau Club, Ottawa, 26 November 1969, vol. 24, UP, LAC; Francis, *Underhill*, 3–4, 174–5.

43 Peter C. Newman, "Frank Underhill – A Good Man with a Great Mind," *Toronto Star*, 27 November 1969.

44 Ramsay Cook, "Un grand intellectuel anglo-canadien," *Le Devoir*, 4 December 1969.

45 CF 50 (April–May 1970): 33.

46 "What Then Is the Manitoban, This New Man? or This Almost Chosen People," Writings 1970, vol. 24, UP, LAC.

47 J.F. Parkinson, "Frank Underhill," CF 51 (November 1971): 7.

48 H. Blair Neatby, "Frank Hawkins Underhill" (obituary notice), *Canadian Historical Review* 52 (December 1971): 480.

EPILOGUE

1 "John Morley," Writings 1945, vol. 19, UP, LAC.

2 Carl L. Becker, *The Heavenly City of the Eighteenth-Century Philosophers* (New Haven: Yale University Press, 1932), 72–3, and Ch. 1, "Climates of Opinion," 1–31.

3 For an interesting take on this reaction, see Christian Caryl, *Strange Rebels: 1979 and the Birth of the 21st Century* (New York: Basic Books, 2013).

4 Mark Kingwell, "Being a Dandy: A Sort of Manifesto," *Queen's Quarterly* 120, no. 1 (Spring 2013): 18–26.

5 Judt, *Ill Fares the Land* (New York: Penguin Books, 2010), 6, 96.

6 James Kloppenberg, *Uncertain Victory: Social Democracy and Progressivism in European and American Thought, 1870–1920* (New York: Oxford University Press, 1986).

7 Judt, *Ill Fares the Land*, 155–6.

8 "Canadian Intellectuals and Politics," 23–4, Writings 1967 [1], vol. 24, UP, LAC.

Index